the food of **Japan**

96 Authentic Recipes from the Land of the Rising Sun

Recipes by Takayuki Kosaki and Walter Wagner
Introduction by Kathleen Morikawa
Food photography by Heinz von Holzen
Styling by Christina Ong

TUTTLE Publishing
Tokyo | Rutland, Vermont | Singapore

T0151614

Published by Tuttle Publishing, an imprint of Periplus Editions (HK) Ltd
www.tuttlepublishing.com

ISBN 978-4-8053-1480-7
Previously published under ISBN 978-4-8053-1003-8

Distributed by

North America, Latin America & Europe

Tuttle Publishing
364 Innovation Drive
North Clarendon, VT 05759-9436 U.S.A
Tel: 1 (802) 773-8930; Fax: 1 (802) 773-6993
info@tuttlepublishing.com
www.tuttlepublishing.com

Japan

Tuttle Publishing
Yaekari Building 3rd Floor
5-4-12 Osaki Shinagawa-ku Tokyo 141-0032
Tel: (81) 3 5437-0171; Fax: (81) 3 5437-0755
sales@tuttle.co.jp
www.tuttle.co.jp

Asia Pacific

Berkeley Books Pte Ltd.
61 Tai Seng Avenue, #02-12, Singapore 534167.
Tel: (65) 6280-1330; Fax: (65) 6280-6290
inquiries@periplus.com.sg
www.periplus.com

All recipes were tested in the Periplus Test Kitchen.

photo credits: All food photography by Heinz von Holzen except
the following: page 12 by Ben Simmons; page 10 by Dallas & John
Heaton; pages 4 and 9 by Eric Oey; page 7 by Photobank.

21 20 19 18   10 9 8 7 6 5 4 3 2 1
Printed in Hong Kong   1804EP

About Tuttle
"Books to Span the East and West"

Our core mission at Tuttle Publishing is to create books
which bring people together one page at a time. Tuttle
was founded in 1832 in the small New England town of
Rutland, Vermont (USA). Our fundamental values remain
as strong today as they were then—to publish best-in-
class books informing the English-speaking world about
the countries and peoples of Asia. The world has become
a smaller place today and Asia's economic, cultural and
political influence has expanded, yet the need for
meaningful dialogue and information about this diverse
region has never been greater. Since 1948, Tuttle has
been a leader in publishing books on the cultures, arts,
cuisines, languages and literatures of Asia. Our authors
and photographers have won numerous awards and
Tuttle has published thousands of books on subjects
ranging from martial arts to paper crafts. We welcome
you to explore the wealth of information available on Asia
at **www.tuttlepublishing.com.**

Contents

Food in Japan

A cuisine designed for all the senses

More than any other cuisine in the world, Japanese food is a complete aesthetic experience—a delight for the eyes, the nose and the palate. The desire to enhance rather than to alter the essential quality of fresh seasonal ingredients results in a cuisine that is unique, a tribute to nature and to man who, after all, produced the exquisite tableware on which the food is presented.

Japanese restaurants abroad were once frequented largely by homesick Japanese tourists or businessmen longing for a taste of home. Over the past few decades, however, Japanese cuisine has earned an international following and inspired the presentation of French *nouvelle cuisine* as well as a wave of Japanese-influenced dishes from Paris to San Francisco to Sydney. As palates become more adventurous and as health-conscious diners seek foods that are low in fat and sugar and make wide use of soy beans and vegetables, Japanese food is becoming increasingly popular and Japanese ingredients are now easier to obtain internationally.

Surrounded by seas, the Japanese have made the bounty of the sea a vital part of their diet, eating a variety of seaweed as well as many different fish and shellfish. The basic stock of Japanese cuisine, *dashi*, is redolent of the sea, being made from dried kelp (*konbu*) and dried bonito flakes.

There is a Japanese saying that a meal should always include "something from the mountain and something from the sea." The mountain being represented by a range of seasonal vegetables together with the staple, rice. Poultry and meat are also eaten, although these are less important than the humble soy bean, which appears as nutritionally rich bean curd (tofu), as miso, fermented soy bean paste used for soups and seasoning, and in the form of the ubiquitous soy sauce.

A number of factors come together to form the main elements of Japanese cuisine. Seasonal and regional specialties set the overall tone for the meal. Historical influences can be seen in the choice of foods, preparation techniques and the custom of eating certain foods at certain times of the year. The presentation of food is of paramount importance, with great care given to detail, color, form and balance. The food provides a showcase for the Japanese arts of porcelain, ceramics, basketware, lacquer and bamboo.

The secret to preparing Japanese cuisine at home is an understanding of a few very simple ingredients and of how a meal is composed; the culinary methods used are actually very easy to master. But the most important requirement of all is simply a love for good food prepared and presented with a sense of harmony.

The Evolution of Japanese Cuisine

Japanese cuisine today is the result of two millennia of culinary influences imported from the outside world, refined and adapted to reflect local preferences in taste and presentation, resulting in a style that is uniquely Japanese.

Rice cultivation, believed to have come from China, began in Japan around 300 B.C. Rice was used as a form of tribute and taxation until the early 20th century, and it became a rare luxury for the farmers who produced it— they had to survive on barley, buckwheat and other grains.

Meat and milk were part of the Japanese diet until the late 7th century. When Buddhism emerged as an important force in the nation, restrictions were placed on meat consumption. In the 8th century, meat-eating was officially prohibited and the forerunner of today's sushi appeared.

Chinese influence on Japanese cuisine continued to be strong for the next three centuries. It was from China that Japan learned the art of making bean curd, and how to use chopsticks. China was also the origin of soy sauce, said to have come from the Asian mainland in the 8th or 9th century, although today's Japanese-style soy sauce is a product of the 15th century. Tea was first introduced from China in the 9th century, but gradually faded from use, only to be reintroduced by a Zen priest in the late 12th century.

OPPOSITE: Early breakfast at a traditional inn on the slopes of Mount Fuji.
BELOW: A tiered lacquer box containing special foods that are served during the first week of the new year.

In the Heian Period (794–1185), Japan's distinctive style of cuisine began to develop. The capital was moved from Nara to Kyoto and the thriving aristocracy had the time to indulge its interests in art, literature, poetry, fine cuisine and elaborate games and pastimes. Elegant dining became an important part of the lifestyle and the aristocracy were not only gourmets but gourmands who supplemented their regular two meals a day with numerous between-meal snacks. Today, *kyo ryori*, the cuisine of Kyoto, represents the ultimate in Japanese dining. This is exemplified by *kaiseki*, which features an assortment of carefully prepared and exquisitely presented delicacies.

In 1885, the government moved to Kamakura where the more austere samurai lifestyle and Zen Buddhism fostered a healthier, simpler cuisine. *Shojin ryori* (vegetar-ian Buddhist temple fare), heavily influenced by Chinese Buddhist temple cooking, features small portions of a wide variety of vegetarian foods prepared using one of the five standard cooking methods. *Shojin ryori* guidelines include placing emphasis on food of five colors (green, red, yellow, white and black-purple) and six tastes (bitter, sour, sweet, hot, salty and delicate). It was an extremely important culinary influence during its time and this emphasis on certain tastes, colors and cooking techniques lives on today. *Shojin ryori* also led to the development of *cha kaiseki*, food served before the tea ceremony, in the mid-16th century.

Japan's trade with the outside world from the 14th to 16th centuries brought many new influences. *Kabocha*, the much-loved, green-skinned pumpkin, was introduced via Southeast Asia by the Portuguese in the 16th century. The

Bitter Sweet

Few things are as quintessentially Japanese as the ritual tea ceremony which, for the non-Japanese, seems to encapsulate all of the mystique, discipline and refinement of Japanese culture. *Cha-no-yu*, the Way of Tea, began in the 15th century and in its early form, placed much emphasis on displaying and admiring imported Chinese art objects.

The Way of Tea gave rise to two of the more interesting aspects of Japanese cuisine: *cha kaiseki*, Japanese haute cuisine designed to be served as a light meal before a tea ceremony, and *wagashi*, traditional Japanese sweets which became an important accessory to the tea ceremony from the mid-16th century on. *Wagashi* today vary from the rather light treats enjoyed with a cup of pale green tea in the afternoon to the exquisitely delicate and often extremely sugary *wagashi* offered to neutralize the bitter taste of the powdered green tea.

Kanten, an agar agar-based gelatin, is an important ingredient in the sweets. When made into a jelly, *kanten* is a pliable sculpting material in the hands of a skilled craftsman who can swiftly carve a pale purple portion of *kanten* into a beautiful hydrangea in full bloom in spring, or create goldfish afloat in a cool sea of jellied *kanten* in summer.

Due to their association with the tea ceremony and the ancient aristocracy, *wagashi* sometimes bear names that allude to the literature and poetry of the distant past.

Although there are some standard favorites available all year-round, most *wagashi* makers vary their products according to the changing seasons. *Sakura mochi*, a soft rice dumpling tinted cherry blossom pink, filled with bean jam and wrapped in a cherry tree leaf, is popular during spring time. *Kashiwa mochi*, a similar cake wrapped in an oak leaf, is eaten in May. Autumn foliage is replicated in October and snow-capped mountain designs take over in winter. In January, the Oriental zodiac's animal for that year makes an appearance.

A visit to a traditional Japanese sweet shop is indeed a treat for the eyes as well as the stomach.

ABOVE: The formal tea ceremony, with its bitter powdered green tea, led to the creation of delicate *wagashi* sweets during the 16th century.
OPPOSITE: An array of tiny portions of exquisitely presented food typical of Japan's haute cuisine, *kaiseki ryori*.

Dutch followed a century later and introduced corn, potatoes and sweet potatoes. European cooking techniques created some interest and developed into what came to be known in Japan as "the cooking of the southern Barbarians" or *nanban ryori*. It is from the Portuguese *pao* that Japan derived its word for bread, *pan*. The Portuguese are credited with introducing tempura (batter-fried foods) as well as the popular cake, *kasutera* (castilla). The culinary cross-cultural communication was not entirely one-sided—the Dutch are rumored to have taken soy sauce back to Europe with them.

During the Edo Period (1603–1857), Japan underwent almost three centuries of self-imposed seclusion from the outside world. The nation looked inward—and a highly refined and very prosperous merchant class with the cash to pursue its sophisticated tastes in food and the arts gradually arose. Noodle restaurants proliferated during this period and *nigiri-zushi* (seasoned rice wrapped in toasted seaweed) was invented.

The Meiji Period (1868–1912) marked the return of contact with the outside world. In the late 19th century, beef was again allowed on the menu, and the early 20th century brought growing interest in foreign treats such as bread, curry, ice cream, coffee and croquettes.

In the postwar period, purists have decried the decline of Japanese home cooking citing the electric rice cooker, instant noodles in styrofoam cups, instant miso soup, powdered *dashi* stock and ready-made pickling preparations that provide "homemade" pickles in minutes. Yet the numerous cooking programs on Japanese television and the number of cookbooks in the bookstores confirm that modern Japanese are still very much interested in the preparation of good food.

The Japanese desire to adapt outside influences to local tastes has never waned and has produced such unique blendings of East and West as green tea ice cream, seaweed-flavored potato chips and cod roe spaghetti. And deep is the shock of the visitor to Japan who bites into a frozen chocolate-colored ice cream, only to discover he has bought an *azuki* or red bean bar instead.

Regional Cooking Styles

The extremes in Japan's climate—from the very cold northern island of Hokkaido to the subtropical islands of Okinawa—result in a range of regional cuisines that are as diverse as the land itself.

In Hokkaido, with its wide open spaces and climate that is not conducive to rice cultivation, people have acquired a taste for potatoes, corn, dairy products, barbecued meats and salmon. Their special version of Chinese noodles, called Sapporo *ramen*, is often served with a dab of butter. Seafood *o-nabe* (one-pot stews) featuring crab, scallops and salmon are also a specialty of the region.

There is a great difference in the food preferences of the residents of the eastern Kanto region (centered around Tokyo and Yokohama) and the western Kansai region (Kyoto, Osaka and environs). In the Kansai area, fermented soy bean soup, or miso, is almost white compared with the darker brown and red miso favored in the Kanto region. Eastern and western Japan are also divided by differing tastes in sushi, sweets and pickles. The Kyoto area is identified with the light, delicately flavored cuisine of the ancient court—true haute cuisine—and many in western Japan feel Tokyoites are a little heavy handed with the soy sauce.

Nagoya, located halfway between Tokyo and Kyoto, is known for its flat *udon* noodles and *uiro*, a sweet rice jelly. Pilgrims visiting the Buddhist temples on Shikoku Island would be sure to try the island's famous Sanuki *udon* noodles, fresh sardines and mandarin oranges. Kyushu Island is known for its tea, fruits and seafood products, and for the Chinese and Western culinary influences that developed because of Nagasaki's role as a center of trade with the outside world. Visitors to Nagasaki make it a point to taste its *kasutera* sponge cake, which is said to be as authentically rich as those made in Spain.

On the subtropical islands of Okinawa, dishes featuring pork are favored. Sweets made with raw sugar, pineapples and papaya are also popular, as are several powerful local drinks: for example, *awamori*, made from sweet potatoes, as well as *habu* sake, a type of liquor that comes complete with a deadly *habu* snake coiled inside the bottle.

A Food for All Seasons

One striking aspect of Japanese cuisine is the emphasis on seasonal cuisine. Every food has its appropriate season, ensuring that Japanese tastes are in harmony with nature, and that the ingredients are the freshest possible.

Connoisseurs delight in the first appearance of any seasonal speciality, and are eager to partake of the first bonito fish or new green tea in spring, or the first mackerel or *matsutake* mushrooms in autumn.

The Japanese year is filled with holidays and festivities that require special seasonal delicacies: appropriate sweets and sweet sake for the Doll Festival parties held for little girls on March 3rd and rice dumplings for moon-viewing parties in September.

The most important of seasonal dining specialities is *osechi ryori*, the special foods that are served during the first week of the new year. Dozens of items are decoratively arranged in tiered lacquer boxes, which are brought out again and again over the first few days of the new year, providing housewives a little respite from the non-stop eating (and serving) that marks the holiday. Customs vary from home to home and region to region, but the typical New Year foods usually include *kamaboko* fish sausages bearing auspicious bamboo, plum and pine designs, *konbu* seaweed rolls tied into bows with dried gourd strips, boiled black beans, chestnuts in a sticky sweet potato paste, herring roe, shredded carrot and white radish in sweet vinegared dressing and pickled lotus root. Vegetables such as shiitake mushrooms, radishes, lotus root, carrots and burdock are boiled in a soy sauce and *dashi* broth. The savory steamed egg custard known as *chawan-mushi* is also often eaten at this time.

Many Japanese mushroom varieties, such as *shimeji*, *enokitake* and shiitake are now widely available outside Japan. Other varieties, such as *matsutake*, are more esoteric and only make a rare appearance in Japanese specialty stores.

A Portable Feast

The *o-bento* or box lunch is a Japanese institution which consists of white rice and an assortment of tiny helpings of meat, fish, vegetables, egg, fruit and a pickled plum (*umeboshi*), all arranged in a small rectangular box.

The pickled plum is believed to aid digestion and is a method of keeping the rice from spoiling. If other ingredients are not available, an *o-bento* may consist only of a red pickled plum planted in the center of a field of white rice; this is called a *Hinomaru bento* or "Rising Sun flag lunch."

Since only small portions of each food are included and a well-balanced variety of foods is necessary, preparing a proper *o-bento* can be a time-consuming ritual. As with almost all Japanese dishes, attention to detail and attractive presentation are paramount.

A homemade *o-bento* is considered a tangible symbol of a wife's or mother's love and devotion. A young husband may be embarrassed by the time and tender loving care devoted to the preparation of the lunch box known as the *aisai bento* ("loving wife's lunch") and be hesitant to eat it in front of colleagues. Children, less easily intimidated, glory and gloat over their lunch boxes. They compare and trade delicacies, demonstrating a sense of security and pride in the love of a mother who will wake at 5 A.M. to fry chicken tidbits, make rectangular omelets, and create panda bear and beagle faces out of seaweed and vegetables.

The most famous of the commercially made *o-bento* are the *ekiben*, the box lunches available at most of the nation's train stations. These vary greatly from one area of the country to another and are considered to be an important way of promoting regional delicacies, customs and crafts. In Takasaki, Gunma Prefecture, a region known for its doll-making industry, the lunch boxes are sold in little red plastic bowls shaped like a Daruma doll, the plastic cover resembling the face of the Daruma. It is a distinctive local touch that has made Takasaki's *ekiben* famous nationwide. For many travelers to Japan, tasting all the different local *ekiben* along their route is no less than a vital part of the trip.

Everyone enjoys an *o-bento* box lunch—from school children and businessmen to Buddhist monks at a temple festival.

The staple accompaniment for these dishes is *o-mochi*, which are rice cakes that can be grilled or boiled in a soup known as *o-zoni*. *O-zoni* and *o-mochi* are traditionally served on New Year's morning. These chewy treats must be eaten carefully, for each year several elderly diners choke to death on their New Year *o-mochi*.

Once, all Japanese families made their own rice cakes, but now it is a tradition that is chiefly maintained in the countryside. *Mochi-gome*, a special type of glutinous rice, is prepared and molded—while it is still hot—into a ball and placed in a large round wooden mortar where the rice is pounded rhythmically. The final product is rolled out into a flat cake and cut into rectangular pieces. In present-day Japan, housewives living in the countryside freeze some of these special cakes, so that they can be defrosted at short notice throughout the year whenever some special occasion arises.

Pastimes and events in the traditional Japanese calender are intimately linked to the related foods of the season, enriching and celebrating the daily rhythm of life. Fruits and vegetables are eaten at the height of their season, or their *shun*, and some fine restaurateurs keep their ears on the ground for the latest news or sighting of the freshest seasonal foods—this never remains a secret for long. Japanese culture continues to be fed by the produce from the forest, seas and fields, prepared skillfully, tastefully and simply.

Cherry blossoms signal the coming of spring, and in top Japanese restaurants, diners may be served a cup of cherry blossom tea with several delicate blossoms floating in the clear, slightly salty beverage. Cherry blossom viewing

parties are a seasonal must for the majority of Japanese. *O-bento* lunch boxes are packed full of delicacies to be eaten beneath the fragrant blossom, although at this time, the emphasis is most often on *o-sake* (the drink) rather than *o-bento* (the food).

Bamboo sprouts are another spring delicacy, as are the year's first bonito and rape blossoms. Spring is also the time when nature lovers take to the forests to hunt for edible wild plants such as bracken (*warabi*) and fiddleheads (*zenmai*).

Summer marks the time for eating grilled eel, which is believed to supply the energy needed to survive the sticky and humid weather. It is also the time for octopus, abalone and plenty of fresh fruits and vegetables, especially the summer favorite, *edamame*—fresh soy beans boiled in the pod, dusted with salt and popped into the mouth as the perfect accompaniment for beer on a hot summer's night. Another summer dining treat is cold noodles served with *dashi* and soy sauce dip.

Strings of persimmon set out to dry can be seen dangling from the eaves of many a farmhouse in the countryside during autumn. This is also the season for roasted chestnuts, soba noodles made from freshly harvested and ground buckwheat, and for mushroom hunting. *Matsutake*, highly prized variety of mushrooms savored for their distinctive fragrance, appear during autumn and connoisseurs crave seasonal soups and rice dishes flavored with this delicacy. *Matsutake* are most prevalent in the cold moun-

tainous areas of central Japan. So greatly valued are the mushrooms that marketing them is a big business in the remote and mountainous areas of Japan, where villagers struggle to defend their crops of "brown gold" from poachers. Their concern is easily understood when one realizes that *matsutake* can be sold for approximately $100 per pound in a normal year.

Late autumn is the best time for preserving the year's vegetable harvest for winter. A large variety of pickling methods are popular in Japan, the most common using miso (fermented soy bean paste), salt, vinegar or rice bran as preservatives.

The onset of winter brings fugu sashimi, strips of raw blowfish which can be a deadly delicacy if the poison in the liver and ovaries is not removed correctly by a licensed chef. Other winter favorites include mandarin oranges and *o-nabe*, one-pot stews designed to warm the body on a cold winter's night. On the final day of the year, it is customary to eat soba, for it is believed that the long noodles will guarantee health and longevity in the new year.

ABOVE: Traditional thatch-roof wooden farmhouses, such as this one in Gifu Prefecture, are increasingly rare in Japan, and therefore have become the focus of special seasonal outings, for example, to view the autumn foliage as shown here. Seasonal foods also play a central role in one's enjoyment of the rustic scenery on these occasions.
RIGHT: Each season has its special foods. Restaurants and private homes change their serving dishes to suit the season, as in this autumnal spread.

Eating and Cooking Japanese Style

For hundreds of years, the Japanese kitchen was a simple dark room with a wood burner, a large crock for holding water, another crock or wooden tub for holding pickles and a wooden counter for cutting. These early kitchens were certainly not bright and pleasant places, but the process of cooking and eating together was made more cheerful by the use of the *irori*, a large open hearth heated with charcoal and positioned in the middle of the main room of the house. A hook above the hearth held a kettle of boiling water for tea, or for one of the one-pot stews that are an important part of Japanese home cooking. Fish and rice cakes were often grilled here too.

The Japanese kitchen took a major step forward in the early postwar period and today, the kitchen is equipped with many modern electrical appliances, including the all-important rice cooker. However, the basic utensils have scarcely changed and most cooks still prefer to use traditional utensils made from bamboo. These include a variety of bamboo baskets for draining noodles (a colander or sieve makes an adequate substitute), a bamboo rolling mat and a bamboo steamer. The bamboo mats, which should be available in any specialty Asian kitchen store, are useful for rolling rice inside wrappers of seaweed (*nori-maki*), for rolling up Japanese omelets, for squeezing the liquid out of cooked vegetables and for a number of other tasks. Tiered bamboo steamers, generally available in Asian stores, can be set above a large saucepan or wok of boiling water.

The average Japanese kitchen will include a mortar and pestle used especially for grinding the sesame seeds that are a vital ingredient in many sauces and dressings (an electric blender is a good substitute). Other important items include a grater for radish, ginger and horseradish; a pan for deep-frying (a wok is ideal); earthenware casserole pots and a variety of sharp knives for cutting meat, vegetables and fish for sashimi.

LEFT: The traditional hearth (*irori*) is now virtually a museum piece in Japan.
ABOVE: A bamboo rolling mat is indispensable in a Japanese kitchen.
RIGHT: The wooden rice scoop and mixing bowl is used to prepare Sushi Rice (page 26)—the scoop is also a symbol of domestic authority.

The most symbolic kitchen utensil, the *shamoji*, (the wooden scoop used to serve rice), has come to represent domestic authority. When an older woman hands over her *shamoji* to her daughter-in-law, she is symbolically expressing her desire to hand over the management of household affairs to the latter, and is also an unspoken admission that the younger woman has finally passed muster.

Planning the Meal

The two extremes of Japanese cuisine are a full *kaiseki ryori*, an exquisite array of a dozen or more tiny portions of food artfully arranged on superb tableware, and the basic meal consisting merely of boiled rice, miso soup and pickles. Japanese cuisine developed out of austerity, and a sense of restraint rather than lavish display is still inherent in Japanese food today. Do not think that because the individual portions of food that make a Japanese meal are small, you will finish the meal hungry. With the wide variety of tastes, textures and flavors, you are certain to feel satisfied at the end of a meal.

The basis of every main meal in Japan is boiled rice, miso soup and pickles. The accompanying dishes are varied according to availability, season, how much time you have for preparation of the meal and so on.

The Japanese do not categorize their food by basic ingredients (for example, vegetables, beef or fish), but by the method with which it is prepared. Food is thus classified as grilled, steamed, simmered, or vinegared. Because this concept is unfamiliar to Western cooks, recipes in this book have been grouped to follow the basic pattern of a Japanese meal.

A Japanese meal can be divided into three main areas: a beginning, a middle and an end. The beginning would include raw fish (sashimi), clear soups and appetizers. The middle of the meal is made

up of a number of seafood, meat, poultry and vegetable dishes prepared by either deep-frying, grilling, steaming, simmering, or serving as a vinegared salad. To ensure variety, each style of preparation would be used only once for the foods making up the middle of the meal. For example, if the fish was deep-fried, the vegetables might be simmered in seasoned stock, the meat grilled and a mixture of egg and savory tidbits steamed. Alternatively, this variety of middle dishes might be replaced by a hotpot (nabe), a one-dish combination which includes ingredients such as seafood, vegetables, meat, bean curd and noodles.

If you are new to Japanese cuisine, you will probably want to keep the menu relatively simple. Thus, planning around the basic soup, pickles and rice, you might like to prepare one appetizer and a couple of other dishes using fish, meat, poultry or vegetables. You might even limit the meal to one simple appetizer and a one-pot dish such as sukiyaki, followed by rice, soup and pickles. As you become more confident, you will find it easier to prepare a greater number of dishes. Do not forget, however, that restraint is a very Japanese characteristic and that it is better to serve three carefully cooked, beautifully presented dishes than six less-than-perfect ones.

The Importance of Presentation

In private homes and many restaurants, all the dishes making up the meal are presented at the same time. At a formal meal, however, the appetizers arrive first, followed by the middle dishes, each served in the order dictated by their method of preparation, concluding with rice, soup, pickles, green tea and fresh fruit.

The presentation of Japanese food is an art that encourages the cook's imagination and creativity. As a German visitor to Japan remarked around the turn of the century, "a person doesn't go to the table as in the West but the table is brought to them from the kitchen already set with food." Individual trays for each diner are set with an assortment of bowls and plates, together with a pair of chopsticks which are finely pointed at the ends (unlike Chinese chopsticks, which are rounded or even blunt at the ends).

The choice of tableware in Japan is influenced by the season as well as by the type of food being served. Restaurants stock four sets of tableware, one for each

season, and even private homes have a wide assortment of tableware in different materials, shapes and sizes. Soup and plain rice are always served in round lacquer bowls with a lid, while basketware is preferred for deep-fried foods. Rustic pottery, fine porcelain, glass, and lacquered trays are all used when considered appropriate.

Generally speaking, foods which are round (such as pieces of rolled meat or slices of lotus root) are presented on rectangular or square plates, while square-shaped foods are likely to be served on round plates. Such imagination is shown in Japan, however, that plates and bowls are not just square, rectangular or round; they might be hexagonal, semi-circular, fan-shaped or resemble a leaf or shell. No wonder a Japanese traveling in Europe in the last century dismissed Western food with the remark "every damn plate is round." It is well worth the effort looking for suitable tableware for your home-cooked Japanese food as it adds enormously to the total aesthetic experience. And just as tableware is important, so too is the garnishing of the food. It has been said in Japan that "a person cannot go out naked in public, neither can food." That carefully placed spray of kinome leaves, that tiny sprig of shiso leaves and flower buds, that bright red ball of grated white radish mixed with grated red chili are all an integral part of the dish.

In most cases, garnishes are edible. When you are using substitutes for garnishes, remember that even if they are similar in color and shape, you will not be able to duplicate the taste of the original ingredient. It is generally not that important to get the exact garnish for particular dishes, so feel free to select garnishes of tiny flowers and leaves that seem to enhance the particular dishes you are serving.

ABOVE: In the West, diners go to the dinner table. In Japan, the "table"—in a form of a tray beautifully set with many different dishes, each one served in a special plate or bowl—is brought to the diners. RIGHT: A cook's imagination and creativity is displayed in the aesthetic presentation of Japanese food, and strict rules govern the serving and eating of a formal Japanese dinner such as this one.

Japanese Ingredients

Alfalfa sprouts are commonly used as a garnish in Japanese cuisine. Always buy fresh alfalfa sprouts—these should be crisp, without brown tips, and preferably consumed shortly after purchase.

Azuki are small red beans that are sold dried. Dried beans need to be soaked before using. *Azuki* beans are cooked, sweetened and sometimes mashed into a paste to make desserts (see page 107). Cooked, sweetened red beans are readily available canned in Asian supermarkets.

Bamboo shoots are available pre-cooked—whole or sliced—in vacuum packs in well-stocked supermarkets. These precooked shoots are crunchy, with a savory sweetness, and are much easier to use than fresh shoots. Fresh shoots have an infinitely superior flavor and texture but need to be boiled for about 2 hours. Canned bamboo shoots are also common, but not as tasty, and should be drained, rinsed and scalded in hot water before use. Unused bamboo shoots should be stored in the refrigerator covered in fresh water for up to 10 days, with the water changed daily.

Bean curd or **tofu** is a healthy and inexpensive source of protein. Several types of bean curd made from soy beans are widely used in Japanese dishes. **Firm tofu** (*momen tofu*) is usually sold packed in water in containers of about 9 oz (250 g) in food stores. It is firmer and easier to handle than fine-textured **silken tofu** (*kinugoshi tofu*), which is usually added to soups or enjoyed chilled. These bean curds are often available in plastic trays or rolls designed to be cut with a sharp knife while still in the plastic so they will keep their shape. **Abura-age** (deep-fried tofu slices) are packaged in plastic packets and are available in the refrigerated section of food stores. The bean curd should be blanched in boiling water and drained to remove excess oil before using.

Benitade are maroon-colored sprouts mainly used as a garnish in most Japanese dishes. They have a slightly peppery taste. They can be substituted with alfalfa sprouts or, for a similar color, finely shredded red cabbage.

Burdock is a long, brown and stick-like root that can measure up to 25 in (60 cm) in length. It is sold as a whole root, or halved. When sliced, a root yields about ½ cup. It should be put into water immediately after scraping off the skin to stop it from discoloring. Nutritious and enjoyed for its texture, fresh burdock is often available in Japanese stores and Asian supermarkets. Canned burdock can be used as a substitute.

Chrysanthemum leaves (*shungiku*) come from a particular variety of the chrysanthemum plant which are edible and enjoyed for their distinctive grassy and slightly bitter flavor. Watercress, spinach or celery leaves make good substitutes if chrysanthemum leaves are not available.

Cloud ear fungus, also known as wood ear fungus, is a crinkly, grayish brown fungus that is available dried, sometimes fresh or presoaked. Dried fungus comes in two sizes, and swells to many times its original size after soaking in warm water.

Daikon is a large white radish which can grow to a length of 15 in (40 cm), with a diameter of about 3 in (8 cm). Choose firm, heavy and unblemished daikons. Widely used in Japanese cooking, the fresh root is often served finely grated and eaten with soy sauce. **Pickled daikon radish** is yellow or white in color, and sold vacuum-packed and in jars.

Dashi stock, made from dried bonito flakes and dried kelp, is the basis of most Japanese soups and sauces. Instant *dashi* can be made from liquid concentrate (*katsuo dashi*), powdered *dashi* granules (*hondashi*) and *dashi* teabags (*dashi-no-moto*) which are sold in plastic packets or glass jars in food stores, and provide a practical alternative when small amounts of *dashi* stock are required. The recipe for Basic Dashi Stock is found on page 23.

Dried bonito flakes (*katsuo bushi*)—along with dried kelp (*konbu*)—are the essential ingredients for making Basic Dashi Stock (page 23). The shavings of bonito fish are available in small plastic packets of varying sizes. The larger ones are used to make *dashi* soup stock whereas the finer ones are used as a garnish. They are readily available in Japanese food stores as well as many supermarkets.

Eggplants used in this book belong to the Japanese variety, which is thin, tender and purple, about 3–4 in (8–10 cm) long. Slender Asian eggplants make good substitutes.

Ginger is widely used as a flavoring for Japanese food. To make ginger juice, finely grate peeled fresh ginger. Squeeze it in a garlic press, or wrap in cheesecloth or muslin and squeeze to extract the juice from 3 in (8 cm) of ginger root. Depending on the age of the ginger (young ginger is juicier), you will obtain 1–2 tablespoons of juice. **Pickled ginger** is eaten as an accompaniment to rice dishes, especially sushi and sashimi. It is made of thin slices of young ginger that have been pickled first in salt, then in vinegar. A pink color is obtained by adding red *shiso* leaves, and sometimes red coloring is also added.

Green tea (*matcha*) is a bitter tea rich in caffeine. The powdered form is used in traditional Japanese tea ceremonies. It is readily available from Japanese stores and is great for making green tea ice cream. To make green tea, whisk ¼ teaspoon of *matcha* powder in ½–1 cup (125–250 ml) warm water.

Japanese cucumbers are short and have a sweeter flavor and a smoother texture than large cucumbers. This variety, also known as Lebanese cucumbers in some countries, is widely available in the fresh vegetables section of food stores. Baby cucumbers or pickling gherkins are good substitutes.

Japanese green peppers are much smaller, and are not spicy. They have a milder flavor than Western bell peppers (capsicum). Generally, 8 Japanese green peppers are equivalent to 1 large bell pepper.

Japanese mustard is quite spicy and is similar to Chinese mustard. It is available prepared in squeeze tubes. Alternatively, canned Japanese mustard powder can be mixed with a little water to form a paste just before use.

Do not substitute with European or American mustards, which are either too sweet or too vinegary.

Japanese rice (*gohan*) is a short-grain variety of rice, which has a somewhat stickier texture than other varieties. Japanese short-grain rice, now grown in California and Australia, is available almost everywhere. Never use fragrant Thai or Basmati rice with Japanese food as they tend not to give good results in Japanese recipes.

Japanese soy sauce (*shoyu*) is brewed from soy beans, wheat and salt, and is saltier than Chinese soy sauce. Chinese soy sauce may be used as a substitute but it is worthwhile to purchase a good quality Japanese soy sauce if you will be cooking much Japanese food. Another type of soy sauce, *tamari*, is black and has a slightly smoky, full-bodied flavor that comes from the addition of wheat. *Tamari* is available in most Japanese stores and well-stocked supermarkets.

Kinome are tender sprigs of the prickly ash tree. The leaves have a decorative appearance and a distinctive taste that makes them a popular garnish during the warmer months. They are readily available in Japanese stores and can be kept refrigerated for about a week. Sprigs of watercress make an acceptable substitute but the flavor is different.

Dried kelp or **konbu**, probably the most important seaweed in Japanese cooking, is an essential ingredient in Basic Dashi Stock (page 23). It has a dark brown color, often with whitish patches of salt and is sold in strips or small folded sheets. Wipe with a damp cloth but do not soak before using. When cooked, it expands into smooth, green sheets which are discarded before serving. 1-in (2½-cm) squares of **salted dried kelp** (*shio-konbu*), available in plastic packets, are either enjoyed as a snack or used as a savory accent in some dishes.

Konnyaku, made from a type of potato, is sold either in powdered form or as grayish brown, jelly-like noodles or blocks kept in plastic packets—these should be stored in water in the refrigerator. Also known as devil's tongue, it has a chewy texture, is bland but is high in minerals with no fat.

Lotus roots have a delicious, crunchy texture and a decorative appearance when sliced, thus making the roots a popular vegetable and garnish in many Japanese dishes. They are sold fresh, covered in mud, or cleaned, in vacuum packs in Asian food stores. The canned version lacks the texture of the fresh root, and should be scalded before use.

Mioga is a pretty, pale pink ginger bud with green tips. Although it is a member of the ginger family, *mioga* is not spicy, unlike most gingers. Only its flower and bud are eaten. The buds are very fragrant when thinly sliced and are used as a garnish, in salads or made into vinegar pickles.

Mirin is a type of sweetened rice wine sold in bottles in Japanese stores.

It is used only for cooking—the alcohol dissipates through cooking. Use 1 teaspoon sugar added to 2 teaspoons sake as a substitute for 1 tablespoon *mirin*.

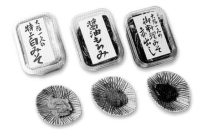

Miso is a protein-rich, salty paste made of fermented soy beans. It has a distinctive aroma and flavor, and is a very important ingredient in Japanese cuisine. Miso must be kept refrigerated and is sold in plastic packs or tubs in the refrigerated section of Asian food stores. It comes in different grades, varieties and colors and the taste ranges from very salty to mild to sweet. The word "miso" used in this book refers to the common brown miso used for soups and sauces and which is easily available in well-stocked supermarkets. **White miso** is actually a light yellow paste, light in flavor and is one of the least salty varieties. White miso is good for both soups and dressings. **Red miso** is reddish brown in color, with an emphatic flavor, and is used for winter soups and stews. Other varieties include **inaka miso** or country miso, which is sweeter and grainier and can be eaten as a dip with fresh vegetables.

Mitsuba, a member of the parsley family, is used as a herb in soups, in salads and with fried foods. Celery leaves or parsley are good substitutes.

Nori, also referred to as laver, is toasted, crisp and sold in very thin, dark green sheets of varying sizes—these sheets are used for wrapping sushi. The sheets used in this book measure 9 x 7 in (23 x 17 cm) pieces, and are packed in bundles of 10. *Nori* is also available as thinly shredded strips or flakes, both of which are used as a garnish served with rice.

Ponzu is a popular Japanese citrus-scented soy sauce dressing available ready mixed in bottles (see page 24). Its main ingredient is the fragrant rind of the *yuzu* orange.

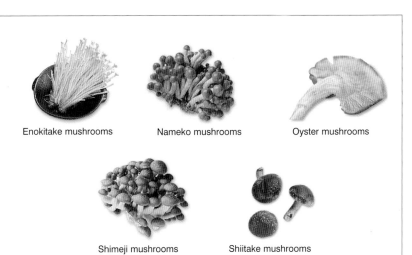

Enokitake mushrooms   Nameko mushrooms   Oyster mushrooms

Shimeji mushrooms   Shiitake mushrooms

Mushrooms are grown commercially, though the mushroom season is eagerly awaited in Japan, as fresh wild mushrooms are highly sought after. Fresh **shiitake mushrooms** have an excellent flavor. **Dried black** or **Chinese black mushrooms** are similar to shiitake mushrooms. **Enokitake mushrooms** or golden mushrooms are clusters of slender cream-colored stalks with tiny caps, and are sometimes available fresh and canned—the tough end of the stems must be discarded before use. Fresh **oyster mushrooms** (*maitake*) are also sold in cans. **Nameko mushrooms** have a slippery texture and attractive reddish brown caps; as their season is short, they are more commonly found in jars or cans. Although rather similar to *nameko* mushrooms in terms of size and shape, **shimeji mushrooms** lack their slippery texture.

Rice vinegar is fermented from rice. Japanese rice vinegar is less acidic than malt or wine vinegars, and has a mild and pleasant fragrance. It is widely available—but slightly diluted cider vinegar or a good quality Chinese rice vinegar, slightly diluted, can be used as substitutes.

Sake or rice wine is available in many different qualities. Besides being popular as a drink, sake is an important ingredient in Japanese cooking. Widely available in liquor stores or in supermarkets where licensing laws do not prevent its sale, it is also sold as cooking sake in Asian supermarkets. Keep refrigerated after opening. Chinese rice wine or very dry sherry are alternatives.

Salted salmon flakes, also known as *shio zake*, is a common ingredient in Japanese rice parcels (*onigiri*), and is also used as a topping for rice. These salted salmon flakes are sold in packets, which are usually available in the refrigerated seafood section of most Japanese supermarkets. Alternatively,

prepare your own by flaking poached salmon and adding a little salt.

Sansho is a peppery powder made from the seeds of the prickly ash tree. *Sansho* powder is available in small glass bottles in Japanese stores. If you cannot find it, freshly ground Sichuan pepper may be used as an acceptable substitute.

Sato-imo potato, also known as taro potato or small baby yam, has a fine creamy texture when well cooked and a subtle, mildly sweet flavor that is slightly different from that of Western potatoes. If *sato-imo* potatoes are not available, use the alternatives given in the recipes in this book.

Sesame seeds come in black and white varieties. The latter is more common, although both types are used in Japan. White sesame seeds are often toasted and crushed to make a paste—you will need 4 tablespoons to make ¼ cup (60 g) of sesame paste. If you do not want to do this yourself, you can buy ready-made

| Udon | Somen | Rice vermicelli |

Noodles are made from various starches (wheat, rice, beans and roots) and are enjoyed both hot and cold in Japan. **Udon**, a common type of wheat flour noodles, comes in various widths and is either flat or round. Packets of dried *udon*, whitish beige in color, are readily found in Japanese stores. **Somen** noodles are also made from wheat, but are very fine and are white in color. **Soba** noodles are made from buckwheat flour. They have a distinctive taste and are sometimes flavored with green tea, in which case their normal beige-brown color is replaced by green. Dried soba noodles are widely available in packets. *Hiyamugi*, or fine white **rice vermicelli** noodles, are identical to the vermicelli used in Chinese cuisine. **Shirataki noodles** are made from *konnyaku* starch and they can be replaced with cellophane or glass noodles, which are made from mung bean flour. Soak them in warm or hot water until they swell and become transparent.

Wakame is a type of seaweed with a pleasant chewy texture and subtle flavor. It is often used in soups and salads. Wakame is sold either dried (it looks like a mass of large crinkly green-black tea leaves) or in salted form in plastic bags. Reconstitute dried seaweed by soaking in water before use. The salted version should be rinsed thoroughly before use.

Wasabi is a pungent root similar in taste to ginger and hot mustard. It is sold fresh, as a prepared paste, or in dried powdered form. Fresh wasabi root should be peeled and grated from the stem top down and should be used within 1–2 days of cutting before it loses its freshness and pungency. The powdered variety may be cheaper, but it is actually powdered horseradish colored green with mustard added. **Wasabi paste** can be made from the powder or the root. Real wasabi is more expensive but has a more potent flavor.

Chinese or Japanese sesame pastes which are usually sold in bottles. Smooth peanut butter makes a good substitute. Middle Eastern tahini, which is slightly bitter, has a different flavor, as the sesame seeds have not been toasted before grinding; add a bit of sugar if you are using tahini as a substitute.

Shiso leaves (also known as perilla leaves) have an attractive dark green color, sometimes with reddish veins, and are widely used in Japanese cooking either as an ingredient or a garnish. It is a member of the mint family, and the leaves have a hint of basil and spearmint flavor. They are crisp-fried as tempura, used to garnish sushi, or minced and added to rice served with sashimi. Decorative sprigs of **shiso flowers** are sometimes used as a garnish.

Whitebait, also known as **silverfish**, *shirauo* or Japanese icefish, is found throughout Japan. This fish grows to a length of about 4 in (10 cm) when fully mature. It is commonly used to make tempura, and may also be added to *chawan-mushi*.

Seven-spice chili powder (*shichimi*) is a mixture of several different spices and flavors. It contains *sansho*, ground chilies, hemp seeds, dried orange peel, flakes of *nori*, white sesame seeds and white poppy seeds. **Shichimi togarashi**, a similar but spicier condiment, consists of several types of chilies and spices. Both are available in small bottles in Japanese stores.

Sour plums or **umeboshi** are salty pickled plums which retain their fruity fragrance. They are very popular with plain rice, eaten as part of breakfast in Japan, and are believed to aid digestion. These dull red plums are available in jars, and should be refrigerated after opening.

Yamato-imo is a type of mountain yam which is grated and used raw for its gluey texture and bright white color. Suitable substitutes are suggested in individual recipes in this book. When cooked, the yam takes on a deliciously soft consistency.

Yuzu oranges have a unique fragrance—reminiscent of lemons, mandarin oranges and limes—which give *ponzu* sauce its distinctive flavor. The essence of *yuzu* is sold in little bottles. Substitute with a very fresh lemon.

Japanese Seafood

Bonito

Bream

Clam

Crab

Flounder

Hairtail Cutlassfish

Half Beak

Lobster

Pufferfish

Redfish

Spanish Mackerel

Squid

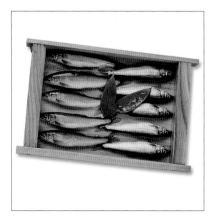

Sweetfish

Tile Fish

Tuna

Whitebait

Whiting

Yellowtail

Preparing Authentic Japanese Recipes

Planning a Japanese Meal

Japanese meals generally consist of many small dishes offering a range of different tastes, colors and textures. A typical meal might include a simple pickle like Pickled Cabbage, Carrot and Cucumber (page 26), a soup like Miso Soup with Mushrooms (page 41), a sushi or sashimi dish (see pages 58–67), accompanied by one or two vegetable or tofu dishes, and white rice, fried rice or noodles. Light dishes are generally served first, followed by heavier dishes. Rice or noodles are served last (see pages 13–14 for more information).

Ingredients

The ingredients used in this book can be found in markets featuring Asian foods, as well as any well-stocked supermarket. Many Japanese ingredients are now available in the condiments and spice section of large supermarkets. When the recipe lists a hard-to-find or unusual ingredient, see pages 16–19 for possible substitutes. If a substitute is not listed, look for the ingredient in your local Asian or Chinese food market, or check the mail-order and website listings on page 112 for possible sources.

The basic ingredients needed to prepare a Japanese meal include sake, Japanese rice, mirin, dried kelp (konbu), rice vinegar, wasabi, nori, Japanese sesame oil and Japanese soy sauce. You may substitute Japanese sesame oil and Japanese soy sauce with the Chinese varieties, even though these do not produce quite the same result. Bonito flakes, used in dashi stock—the ubiquitous stock base for soups and sauces—are another essential ingredient. If bonito flakes are unavailable, use instant dashi stock granules.

Always buy short-grain Japanese rice for an authentic Japanese meal. This variety is stickier than other long-grain varieties. As Japanese cuisine places such emphasis on the freshness of the ingredients, be sure to purchase the necessary items on the day of cooking.

Portions

Japanese meals are often served in individual portions, as main dishes and condiments are normally placed on a tray set before the diner. However, there are dishes, especially the one-pot dishes, that are consumed in a group. As a general rule, the recipes in this book will serve 4–6 people.

Basic equipment

Japanese food preparation methods are very simple, and just a few basic utensils are needed to produce an authentic Japanese meal. The essential equipment includes a rice cooker, a cutting board, a sharp knife, Japanese chopsticks (hashi)—these differ from Chinese chopsticks, as they are thinner and more pointed at the ends—a bamboo mat for rolling sushi (makisu) and a Japanese grater (oroshigane). If you plan to serve Japanese food regularly, you may want to buy a set of Japanese-style tableware, which consists of plates of varying shapes, individual saucers as well as soup and garnish bowls.

Soup Stocks

Basic Dashi Stock

1 strip dried kelp (konbu), (4 in/10 cm long), wiped with a damp cloth
4 cups (1 liter) water
4 cups (50 g) dried bonito flakes

Soak the dried kelp in a saucepan of water for 1 hour. Simmer over medium heat. Just before the water comes to a boil, remove and discard the kelp. Sprinkle the bonito flakes into the water and remove the saucepan from the heat immediately. As soon as the flakes sink, strain the stock and discard the flakes.

Note: The stock keeps refrigerated for 3 days. To make instant dashi from granules (hondashi), add ½ teaspoon dashi stock granules to 1 cup (250 ml) hot water. The granules contain salt, so taste before adding the full amount of salt called for in the recipes.

Yields 4 cups
Preparation time: 7 mins
Cooking time: 7 mins

Cold Soba Dashi Broth

1 cup (250 ml) Basic Dashi Stock (above)
2 tablespoons Japanese soy sauce
¼ cup (60 ml) mirin

Place all ingredients in a saucepan, bring just to a boil over medium heat and remove from the heat immediately. Serve with cold soba noodles. Keeps refrigerated for up to 4 days.

Yields 1¼ cups
Cooking time: 7 mins

Sauces and Batters

Ponzu Dipping Sauce

1 strip dried kelp (*konbu*), (about 2 in/
 5 cm long), wiped with a damp cloth
⅓ cup (85 ml) *yuzu* orange, or lemon
 or lime juice
⅓ cup (85 ml) Japanese soy sauce
2 tablespoons *mirin*
1½ tablespoons *tamari* or dark soy
 sauce
2 tablespoons Basic Dashi Stock
 (page 23) or ¼ teaspoon *dashi*
 stock granules dissolved in
 2 tablespoons hot water

Heat the dried kelp over a gas flame
or under a broiler (grill) until crisp
and fragrant, then put in a bowl or
jar with all the other ingredients. Cover
and refrigerate for 3 days, then strain.
Can be stored for up to a year.

Bottled *yuzu* juice and ready-
made *ponzu* sauce can be
purchased in Japanese stores.

Yields 1 cup   Preparation time: 5 mins

Sukiyaki Sauce

6 tablespoons Japanese soy sauce
5 tablespoons *mirin*
5 tablespoons sake
5–6 tablespoons sugar
1½ cups (375 ml) chicken stock or
 1½ cups (375 ml) Basic Dashi Stock
 (page 23) or ¾ teaspoon *dashi*
 stock granules dissolved in 1½ cups
 (375 ml) hot water

Combine all the ingredients in a
pan and bring to a boil, stirring to
dissolve the sugar. Once the sugar
is dissolved, remove from the heat
and pour the sauce into a bowl.

Yields 2½ cups
Preparation time: 5 mins
Cooking time: 5 mins

Sesame Dipping Sauce
Goma Tare

5 tablespoons white sesame seeds
1 tablespoon miso
2 tablespoons *mirin*
1 tablespoon *tamari* or dark soy sauce
1 tablespoon Japanese soy sauce
1 tablespoon freshly squeezed lemon
 juice or rice vinegar
½ tablespoon sugar
½ teaspoon grated young ginger
¼ teaspoon ground red pepper
¼ cup (85 ml) water

Dry-roast the white sesame seeds in
a skillet until light golden brown. Do
not burn the seeds or it will taste bitter. Place the warm toasted seeds
and all the other ingredients in a
blender. Sesame Dipping Sauce is
best prepared a day ahead for the
flavors to blend. Keeps refrigerated
for 2 to 3 days.

Yields ½ cup   Preparation time: 5 mins

Tosa Vinegar   Tosa-zu

½ cup (125 ml) water
1 strip dried kelp (*konbu*), (about 2 in/
 5 cm long), wiped with a damp cloth
⅓ cup (85 ml) rice vinegar
2 teaspoons Japanese soy sauce
1 tablespoon *mirin*
1½ tablespoons sugar
¼ teaspoon salt
½ tablespoon dried bonito flakes

Pour the water with the dried kelp,
vinegar, soy sauce and *mirin* into
a saucepan and heat. Just before
the mixture boils, remove the kelp
and add the sugar and salt. Stir
well to dissolve and bring to a simmer. Remove from the heat and
add the bonito flakes. Set aside to
cool, then strain and discard solids.
Keeps refrigerated for up to a week.

Yields ¾ cup   Preparation time: 10 mins
Cooking time: 7 mins

Sweet Vinegar   Amazu

1 cup (250 ml) water
½ cup (125 ml) rice vinegar
⅓ cup (60 g) sugar
1 teaspoon salt

Bring the water and vinegar to a boil
in a saucepan, then add the remaining ingredients and stir to dissolve
the sugar and salt. Remove from
the heat and set aside to cool. Use
for dipping and pickling vegetables.
Keeps refrigerated for up to 10 days.

Yields ½ cup   Preparation time: 4 mins

Chicken Yakitori Glaze
Tori Tare

½ cup (125 ml) chicken stock or
 ½ teaspoon chicken stock powder
 dissolved in ½ cup (125 ml) water
⅓ cup (85 ml) sake
½ cup (125 ml) *mirin*
½ cup (125 ml) Japanese soy sauce
2 tablespoons sugar

Place all the ingredients into a
small saucepan and bring to a
boil. Reduce heat and simmer for
20 minutes, or until the sauce is
reduced to half the original volume.
The sauce keeps refrigerated for up
to 1 month. Use this sauce for brushing when grilling chicken yakitori.

Yields ¾ cup   Preparation time: 5 mins
Cooking time: 25 mins

Teriyaki Sauce

1 cup (250 ml) Japanese soy sauce
1 cup (250 ml) sake
1½ cups (375 ml) *mirin*
5–6 tablespoons sugar

Combine all the ingredients in a
saucepan and bring to a boil over
medium heat. Simmer on medium-
low heat, stirring constantly, until the
sauce is reduced to less than half
the original volume. Keeps refrigerated for 6 months.

Yields 1¼ cups   Cooking time: 30 mins

Japanese Mayonnaise
Tamago-no-moto

2 egg yolks
½ teaspoon lemon juice
½ cup (125 ml) salad oil
1 tablespoon white miso
Pinch of salt and white pepper
Pinch of grated *yuzu*, lime or lemon
   peel (optional)

Beat the egg yolks and lemon juice
in a bowl using a wooden spoon.
Continue beating, adding the salad
oil a few drops at a time until the
mixture begins to emulsify. Continue
until all the oil is used up, then stir
in the miso and season with salt,
pepper and grated peel, if using.

Yields ¾ cup   Preparation time: 25 mins

Sashimi Soy Dip
Tosa Shoyu

3 tablespoons sake
½ cup (125 ml) Japanese soy sauce
2 tablespoons *tamari* soy sauce
   or *mirin*
1 strip dried kelp (*konbu*), (about 2 in/
   5 cm long), wiped with a damp cloth
½ cup (5 g) dried bonito flakes

Place all the ingredients in a small
saucepan and simmer on medium-
low heat for 5 minutes. Allow to
cool, then strain and discard solids.
The sauce can be stored for up to a
year if kept refrigerated in a jar. Use
as a dipping sauce for sashimi.

Yields ¾ cup   Preparation time: 5 mins
Cooking time: 5 mins

Tempura Batter
Tempura Ko

1 egg yolk
1 cup (250 ml) ice water
1 cup (150 g) cornstarch, sifted

Put the egg yolks in a bowl and
mix in the water gradually. Add the
cornstarch all at once and stir briefly
(preferably with a pair of chopsticks).
Tempura batter should be thin and
lumpy. It is best made just before
cooking, however the batter can be
refrigerated until required.

Yields 2 cups   Preparation time: 5 mins

Sushi Rice   Sushi-Meshi

1 cup (200 g) uncooked Japanese
   rice (yields 2 cups of cooked rice)
1¼ cups (310 ml) water
1 strip dried kelp (*konbu*), (4 in/10
   cm long), wiped with a damp cloth
   and quartered

Dressing
2 tablespoons rice vinegar
1 tablespoon sake
2 teaspoons sugar
1 teaspoon salt

Rinse the rice gently and drain or
see packet instructions. Cook the
rice, water and kelp in a saucepan
and bring almost to a boil over
high heat. Reduce the heat, discard
the kelp, and simmer, covered, for
15 minutes until the rice is cooked.
Turn the heat off, remove the lid
and cover the pan with a towel to
absorb condensation. Set aside
for 20 minutes. Stir the Dressing
ingredients in a non-reactive bowl
to dissolve the sugar. Set aside.
Put the cooked rice in a wide

wooden tub or large bowl. Add
the Dressing and stir gently in a
circular motion with a rice paddle
or wooden spoon. Ideally, the rice
mixture should be fanned to help
cool it. Cover the rice with a damp
cloth until ready to use. Do not
refrigerate. Keep at room temperature and use within 4 hours.

Yields 2 cups
Preparation time: 10 mins (+ 1 hour
for draining rice)
Cooking time: 40 mins

Pickles

Pickled Eggplant
Nasu No Shiomomi

8 oz (250 g) Japanese eggplants,
  washed, halved lengthwise and cut
  into ½ in (1 cm) slices
2 teaspoons salt
Toasted sesame seeds, crushed,
  to garnish (optional)

Sprinkle the eggplants with the
salt and set aside for 10 minutes.
Squeeze gently in a muslin cloth to
remove moisture. Serve garnished
with the sesame seeds.

Yields 1 cup
Preparation time: 15 mins

Pickled Ginger   Gari

8 oz (250 g) young ginger, peeled
  and thinly sliced diagonally
⅓ cup (85 ml) rice vinegar
2 tablespoons *mirin*
2 tablespoons sake
5 teaspoons sugar

RInse the ginger slices thoroughly
and blanch in boiling water and set
aside to drain. Add the rest of the
ingredients into a saucepan and
bring to a boil, stirring to dissolve the
sugar. Set aside to cool. Place the
ginger in a sterilized jar and pour
the vinegar mixture over it. Cover
and keep for 3–4 days before using.
The ginger keeps well refrigerated
for 1 month—it may develop a pale
pink color as it ages. Serve with
sushi and other Japanese dishes.

Yields 1 cup
Preparation time: 20 mins
Cooking time: 5 mins

Pickled Cabbage, Carrot and Cucumber

1 small Japanese cucumber
1 small carrot, washed and peeled
2 cabbage leaves, washed and
  drained, cut into small pieces
1½ teaspoons salt
Toasted sesame seeds, to garnish
  (optional)

Rub ½ teaspoon of the salt onto the
cucumber skin. Rinse and pat dry.
Then, halve the cucumber lengthwise and slice into matchsticks,
slice the carrots the same way.
Add the remaining salt to all the
ingredients and mix gently. Transfer
to a covered container and leave
overnight. Garnish with the sesame
seeds before serving.

Yields 2 cups
Preparation time: 20 mins

Daikon Pickled in Miso
Kabu No Misozuke

14 oz (400 g) daikon radish (about
  6 in/15 cm), washed, peeled,
  halved lengthwise
1 teaspoon salt
½ cup (100 g) *inaka* miso
2 tablespoons sake
4 teaspoons sugar

Sprinkle the daikon with the salt and
set aside for 2–3 hours. Squeeze
gently in a muslin cloth to remove
moisture. Mix the miso, sake and
sugar until the sugar dissolves.
Coat the daikon with the miso mixture and set aside to marinate for 3
hours. Remove the daikon from the
marinate and slice into thick wedges.

Yields 1 cup
Preparation time: 15 mins

Garlic Pickled in Miso
Ninniku Miso-zuke

3 bulbs garlic (5 oz/150 g), cloves
  peeled and left whole
1 teaspoon salt
5 tablespoons *inaka* miso
4 tablespoons sugar

Sprinkle the garlic with the salt and
set aside for 3 hours. Pat dry with
paper towels. Mix the miso and
sugar until the sugar dissolves. Add
the garlic cloves and set aside to
marinate for 4 days before serving.

Yields ¾ cup
Preparation time: 15 mins

Shiba-zuke Pickles
Shiba-zuke

1 Japanese cucumber (3 oz/90 g)
1 small eggplant (3 oz/90 g)
2 teaspoons salt
1 *mioga* or torch ginger bud
½ teaspoon Japanese soy sauce

Rub ½ teaspoon of the salt onto the
cucumber skin. Rinse and pat dry.
Then, halve the cucumber lengthwise and cut into wedges. Sprinkle
with ½ teaspoon salt, mix and set
aside. Halve the eggplant lengthwise and cut into wedges. Sprinkle
with ½ teaspoon salt, mix and set
aside. Thinly slice the *mioga* bud
diagonally, mix with ½ teaspoon
salt and set aside. Place the salted
vegetables and soy sauce in a
bowl, mix well and cover with a lid
and a weight to press. Set aside for
half a day. The pickles can be kept
refrigerated for 3 days.

Yields 1 cup
Preparation time: 15 mins

Mixed Chicken and Vegetable Yakitori

These skewers of grilled chicken and vegetables are very popular both in Japan and abroad.

10 oz (300 g) boneless chicken thighs, cubed
2 leeks, cut into lengths
4 oz (125 g) chicken livers, halved
8 fresh shiitake mushrooms, stems discarded and caps halved
12 small Japanese green peppers or 2 large bell peppers, deseeded and cut into strips
6 stalks asparagus, cut into lengths
36 bamboo skewers, soaked in water for 1 hour before grilling
Oil, to baste
1 portion Chicken Yakitori Glaze (page 24)

Chicken Meatballs
10 oz (300 g) ground chicken
2 teaspoons sugar
2 teaspoons Japanese soy sauce
1 teaspoon fresh ginger juice
1 egg, lightly beaten
2 teaspoons bread crumbs
2 teaspoons cornstarch
4 cups (1 liter) Basic Dashi Stock (page 23) or 2 teaspoons *dashi* stock granules dissolved in 4 cups (1 liter) hot water
3 tablespoons sake

Condiments
Seven-spice chili powder (*shichimi*)
Sansho pepper powder
1 lemon, cut into wedges

1 Prepare the Chicken Yakitori Glaze following the instructions on page 24.
2 Prepare the Chicken Meatballs by combining the ground chicken with the sugar, soy sauce, ginger juice, egg, bread crumbs and cornstarch, mixing well. Scoop 1 tablespoon of the chicken mixture and shape into small meatballs, ¾ in (2 cm) in diameter. Bring the *dashi* stock and sake to almost a boil. Gently drop the chicken meatballs into the simmering stock, a few at a time, and simmer until the meatballs change color. Thread the meatballs onto the skewers. Reserve the stock.
3 Alternate the pieces of chicken thigh and leek onto skewers and set aside. Thread the chicken livers onto skewers and set aside. Thread all the vegetables onto skewers and brush lightly with oil and set aside.
4 Heat up a charcoal barbecue or grill and cook the prepared skewers. When the skewered chicken, meatballs and livers are half-cooked, brush with the yakitori glaze and return to the grill briefly. Baste the food a couple more times during cooking, but take care not to overcook. Sear the vegetables quickly on the grill until done.
5 Strain the *dashi* stock and serve together with the yakitori, if desired. Serve with the range of Condiments.

Serves 8–10   Preparation time: 30–45 mins   Cooking time: 10 mins

Grilled Bean Curd Topped with Miso   Tofu Dengaku

Small blocks of fresh tofu topped with three different types of miso make a colorful and unusual appetizer.

2 cakes firm tofu (about 1 lb/500 g)

Miso Toppings
6 tablespoons white miso
3 tablespoons sake
3 tablespoons *mirin*
1 tablespoon sugar
½ teaspoon very finely grated *yuzu* orange or lemon peel
⅓ cup (10 g) *kinome*, watercress, parsley leaves or spinach leaves

Red Dengaku Miso
3 tablespoons red miso
1½ tablespoons sake
1½ tablespoons *mirin*
½–1 tablespoon sugar
1 tablespoon water

1 Remove the excess moisture from the tofu by wrapping it in a clean cloth and placing it between two cutting boards for 20 minutes. Cut the tofu into half horizontally and then into quarters to obtain rectangular strips.
2 Prepare the three miso toppings. Make the light yellow and green Miso Toppings by combining the miso, sake, *mirin* and sugar in a saucepan and bring almost to a boil. Reduce heat and simmer for 5 minutes, stirring well to dissolve the sugar. Divide the mixture into two bowls.
3 Add the grated citrus peel to one bowl, stir and set aside.
4 To make the green topping. Grind the greens using a mortar and pestle or finely mince. Squeeze to obtain a small quantity of green juice. Add this green juice to the other bowl of the miso mixture. Stir and set aside.
5 For the red topping, put the ingredients for the Red Dengaku Miso in a small saucepan. Bring almost to a boil. Reduce heat and simmer for 5 minutes, stirring well to dissolve the sugar. Remove from the heat and set aside.
6 Grill the pieces of tofu under a broiler for 1 minute until lightly browned on both sides. Spread each piece of tofu with one of the three toppings and return to the grill briefly until brown on top. If you like, carefully insert a skewer into each tofu rectangle as shown. Serve hot.

Serves 6–8   Preparation time: 30 mins   Cooking time: 15 mins

Braised Burdock and Carrot   Kinpira Gobo

8 oz/250 g burdock root (about 1¼ whole roots)
1 large or 2 small carrots (about 4 oz/125 g)
½ cup (100 ml) Basic Dashi Stock (page 23) or ½ teaspoon *dashi* stock granules dissolved in ½ cup (125 ml) hot water
3 teaspoons sugar
1½ tablespoons Japanese soy sauce
1 tablespoon cooking oil
½ teaspoon sesame oil
¼ teaspoon seven-spice chili powder (*shichimi*), to taste
1 teaspoon sesame seeds, dry-roasted in a pan until golden brown

1 Scrape the skin off the burdock with the back of a knife. Slice the burdock into sections, then into matchsticks and immerse in water. Peel and cut the carrot to approximately the same size as the burdock.
2 Combine the *dashi* stock and sugar in a pan and heat until the sugar has dissolved. Add the soy sauce and set aside.
3 Heat the oil in a wok or frying pan and stir-fry the burdock for 1 minute until it is half-cooked. Add the carrot strips and stir-fry for 30 seconds until they are well coated with the oil. Pour in the *dashi* stock and simmer for 1 to 2 minutes until the vegetables are barely cooked and still crunchy. Sprinkle with the sesame oil. Stir to mix well.
4 Transfer to four serving bowls, then sprinkle with a little seven-spice chili powder and sesame seeds. Serve at room temperature.

Serves 4   Preparation time: 20 mins   Cooking time: 12 mins

Simmered Butternut Squash or Pumpkin   Kabocha No Nimono

Pumpkin and butternut squash are very popular in Japan, not only for their sweet taste but also for their beautiful bright orange color. This recipe works best with butternut squash, although any type of pumpkin or winter squash with a strong flavor and dense flesh may be used.

2½ cups butternut squash or pumpkin (about 1 lb/500 g), washed and cut in half
1 cup (250 ml) Basic Dashi Stock (page 23) or ½ teaspoon *dashi* stock granules dissolved in 1 cup (250 ml) hot water
½–1 tablespoon sugar
2 tablespoons Japanese soy sauce

1 Remove the seeds from the squash or pumpkin and scoop out any fibers with a spoon. Cut into chunks, and peel off the skin on the edges of each piece, leaving a bit of the skin intact so that the squash or pumpkin holds its shape during cooking. You can also cut it into decorative shapes as shown in the photo if desired.
2 Pour the *dashi* stock and sugar into a pan and bring to a boil. Add the pumpkin and simmer gently for 7 to 8 minutes. Turn the pieces over, add the soy sauce and continue cooking until the vegetable is tender. Divide into individual serving bowls. Serve warm, with a little of the cooking liquid poured into each bowl.

Serves 4   Preparation time: 5 mins   Cooking time: 10 mins

Green Bean Salad with Tart Sesame Dressing   Ingen Goma-Ae

10 oz (300 g) french beans
Finely shredded *nori*, to garnish

Tart Sesame Dressing
4 tablespoons ground sesame paste
½ tablespoon Japanese soy sauce
½ teaspoon salt
1 tablespoon sugar
1 tablespoon rice vinegar or lemon juice
2 tablespoons Basic Dashi Stock (page 23) or ¼ teaspoon *dashi* stock granules dissolved in 2 tablespoons hot water

1 Blanch the beans in a saucepan of lightly salted water for about 2 to 3 minutes until just tender. Drain and cool under cold running water, then slice into lengths.
2 Mix the Tart Sesame Dressing ingredients in a bowl. Divide the beans into four serving bowls, top each with a spoonful of the dressing and garnish with the shredded *nori*.

Note: Substitute ground sesame paste with tahini or peanut butter. If using tahini, increase the amount of sugar and lemon juice by ½ tablespoon called for in the recipe. If using peanut butter, use ½ tablespoon sugar and 1½ tablespoons lemon juice.

Serves 4   Preparation time: 20 mins   Cooking time: 10 mins

Spinach with Sesame Sauce   Horenso Goma

This simple but tasty appetizer is served at room temperature and may be prepared well in advance.

10 oz (300 g) spinach, washed and
    left whole, thick stems removed
4 cups (1 liter) water
1 tablespoon salt
3 tablespoons sesame seeds
1 tablespoon sugar
2 tablespoons Basic Dashi Stock
    (page 23) or ½ teaspoon *dashi*
    stock granules dissolved in 2
    tablespoons hot water
Nori strips, to wrap
Thin *nori* strips, to garnish

1 Bring the water and salt to a boil. Lightly blanch the spinach leaves until they are soft but not soggy. Drain in a colander and cool under running water. Drain again, pressing on the spinach with your hands or the back of a wooden spoon to remove excess water. Lay the spinach on a bamboo rolling mat and roll up tightly to squeeze out any remaining moisture and shape into a roll.
2 Dry-roast the sesame seeds in a skillet until light golden brown, stirring constantly. Take care not to burn the seeds as this would them taste bitter. Grind, using a mortar and pestle or a spice grinder, to a coarse, grainy paste. Add the sugar and *dashi* stock to smoothen the mixture into a creamy paste.
3 Just before serving, slice the rolled spinach into short sections. Wrap the *nori* strip around the spinach like a belt and top each bundle with a little sesame sauce and sprinkle with the shredded *nori*.

Serves 4   Preparation time: 10 mins   Cooking time: 10 mins

Seaweed and Cucumber Salad   Mozuku

The chewy texture of *mozuku*, a hair-like seaweed, combined with the rather viscous *yamato* potato garnish makes an unusual appetizer. Substitute *yamato* potato with slices or finely grated hard-boiled eggs. This recipe also works really well with the easily available *wakame* seaweed and sliced cucumber.

200 g (7 oz) drained water-packed
    mozuku seaweed, or 5 tablespoons
    dried *mozuku* seaweed
2 tablespoons peeled and finely
    grated *yamato* potato, 4 hard-boiled
    quail eggs, or 1 hard-boiled egg,
    sliced
1 cup (250 ml) Tosa Vinegar
    (page 24)
2 teaspoons very finely grated young
    ginger
4 sprigs *kinome*, watercress or parsley
Gold powder, to garnish (optional)

1 If using the dried and salted seaweed, soak the seaweed in water for 1 hour to remove salt. Then rinse thoroughly in a sieve, and scald with hot water. Drain and set aside.
2 Mix the seaweed, potato and vinegar, then portion into four individual bowls. Serve garnished with the grated *yamato* potato or egg. Top with a pinch of ginger, *kinome* and gold powder (if using).

Note: To make **Wakame and Cucumber Salad**, use 3 tablespoons dried *wakame* seaweed, rinsed and soaked in water to soften, drain and set aside. Rub ½ teaspoon of the salt onto the skin of 2 Japanese cucumbers. Rinse the salt off. Then, slice thinly on the diagonal, sprinkle with another ½ teaspoon salt and mix well. Rinse the cucumber slices in cold water and squeeze gently. Mix the cucumber with the *wakame* seaweed then add 1 cup Tosa Vinegar, and toss. Serve chilled, garnished with strips of finely sliced young ginger.

Serves 4   Preparation time: 15 mins

Mixed Grilled Seafood Appetizer Sumi-Yaki

The sweetness of very small whiting or other small white-fleshed fish is excellent, but if small white fish are not available, fillets of any white fish can be used in this simple combination of grilled food.

1 lb (500 g) white fish fillets or small whole fish like Japanese whiting
½ teaspoon salt
8 fresh medium shrimp
8 small Japanese green peppers, or 1 large bell pepper, cut into 8 strips
8 fresh shiitake mushrooms, stems discarded, caps left whole
Oil, to brush on the bell peppers

Accompaniments
1 cup (250 ml) Ponzu Dipping Sauce (page 24), divided into individual serving bowls
4 oz (125 g) daikon radish (about 2 in/5 cm), finely grated
1 lemon, cut into 8 wedges

1 If using whole fish, clean, scale and slice each one open lengthwise. Sprinkle the fish with salt and set aside to air-dry for 1 hour. In the meantime, peel and devein the shrimp, discarding the heads but leaving the tails intact.
2 Make a small slit in the sides of each Japanese green pepper (if using). Brush the green pepper with a little oil.
3 Grill or broil all ingredients under high heat, for about 3 minutes on each side. Serve with individual saucers of Ponzu Dipping Sauce, grated daikon and lemon wedges.

Serves 4–6   Preparation time: 10 mins   Cooking time: 7 mins

Grilled Eggplant Salad with Ginger and Bonito Flakes Yaki Nasu

Charcoal-grilled eggplant has an incomparable flavor—enhanced in this recipe by the delicately seasoned *dashi* stock.

1 lb (500 g) slender Japanese eggplants
4 tablespoons Basic Dashi Stock (page 23) or ¼ teaspoon *dashi* stock granules dissolved in 4 tablespoons hot water
1 tablespoon Japanese soy sauce
1 in (2½ cm) young ginger, grated
½ cup (5 g) dried bonito flakes, to garnish

1 Prick the skin of the eggplants in a few places with a toothpick to prevent them from bursting during cooking. Grill the eggplants under a very hot broiler or grill, turning frequently until the skins are slightly blackened and the flesh is soft.
2 Remove from the grill, plunge into a basin of cold water, drain and peel off the skins. Cut the eggplant into strips lengthwise or crosswise into sections.
3 Combine the *dashi* stock and soy sauce in a bowl. Arrange the eggplants on individual serving plates and drizzle with a bit of the sauce mixture. Top with grated ginger and sprinkle with bonito flakes.

Serves 4   Preparation time: 10 mins   Cooking time: 5–8 mins

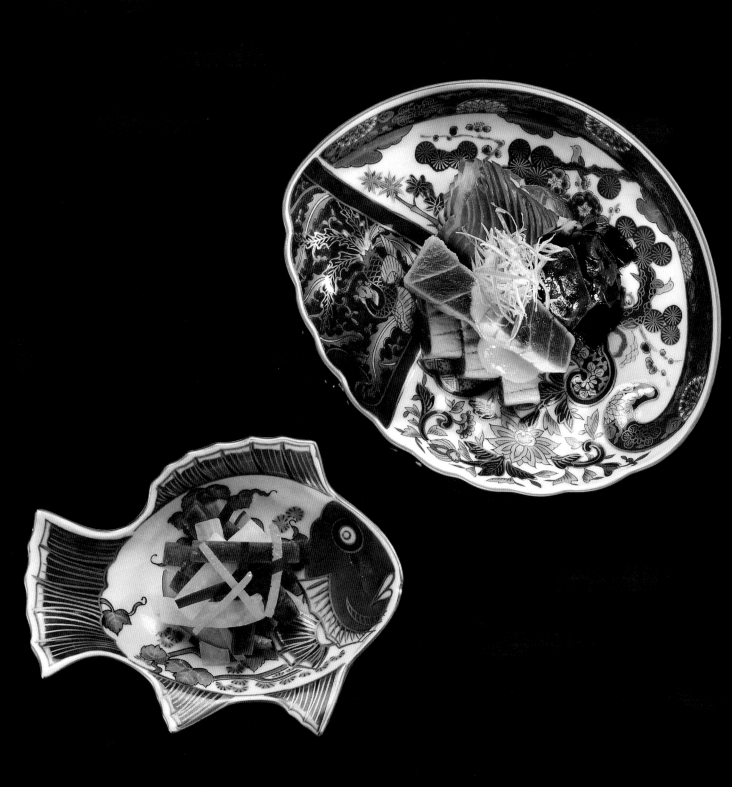

Fresh Seared Tuna with Seaweed and Cucumber Salad

Nuta

An excellent combination of lightly seared or blanched tuna (the outside cooked for a few seconds while the inside is still raw), crunchy cucumber slices and chewy *wakame* seaweed.

8 oz (250 g) fresh sashimi-grade tuna
Oil, to sear
1½ heaped tablespoons dried *wakame* seaweed, rinsed and soaked in water to soften
1 small Japanese cucumber
1 teaspoon salt
1 *mioga* or spring onion, white part only, thinly sliced, to garnish

Miso Mustard Dressing
5½ tablespoons white miso
1½ teaspoons sesame paste or smooth peanut butter
2½ tablespoons rice vinegar
½–1 tablespoon sugar
2 teaspoons Japanese soy sauce
1–2 teaspoons prepared Japanese mustard paste

1 In a small bowl, mix all the ingredients for the Miso Mustard Dressing and set aside.

2 Heat a skillet with a few drops of oil and lightly sear the tuna for a few seconds on all sides. Alternatively, boil a cup of water in a saucepan. Using a pair of chopsticks, plunge the tuna in the boiling water for 5 to 10 seconds until the flesh on the outside starts to turn pinkish white. Remove and chill in ice water for a few seconds, drain and cut into sashimi-thin slices.

3 Rub ½ teaspoon of the salt onto the cucumber skin. Then, halve the cucumber lengthwise and cut into paper-thin strips. Sprinkle with the remaining salt, mix and set aside for 5 minutes. Rinse off the salt and gently squeeze out the moisture.

4 Arrange the tuna, *wakame* and cucumber on a platter. Top with a little of the dressing and garnish each serving with strips of *mioga* or spring onion.

Serves 4   Preparation time: 15 mins   Cooking time: 5 mins

Daikon and Carrot Salad with Sweet Vinegar Dressing

Namasu

This colorful and simple salad with a sweet vinegar dressing is a traditional Japanese New Year dish.

7 oz (200 g) daikon radish (about 3 in/8 cm)
1 small carrot (about 5 oz/150 g)
2 small Japanese cucumbers
1 teaspoon salt
1 strip dried kelp (*konbu*), (3 in/8 cm long), wiped with a damp cloth
½ cup (125 ml) Sweet Vinegar (page 25)
Yuzu orange or lemon peel, grated, to garnish (optional)

1 Cut the daikon and carrot into thin, rectangular, matchstick-length slices. Sprinkle with the salt and rub it in with your fingers. Rinse the vegetables under running water, drain, squeeze gently and set aside.

2 Rub ½ teaspoon of the salt onto the cucumber skin. Then, halve the cucumber lengthwise and cut into paper-thin strips. Sprinkle with the remaining salt, mix and set aside for 5 minutes. Rinse off the salt and gently squeeze out the moisture.

3 Wipe the dried kelp with a damp cloth, then cut into very fine shreds with a pair of scissors. Place the shredded kelp in a small bowl and soak with a little of the Sweet Vinegar. Set aside for 20 minutes. In another bowl, add the daikon, carrot and the remaining Sweet Vinegar, and set aside for 20 minutes.

4 Drain the daikon and carrot, and arrange on a plate. Top with the soaked kelp, garnish with the peel and serve.

Serves 4–6   Preparation time: 15 mins

Miso Soup with Mushrooms   Tofu To Nameko No Miso Shiru

Nameko mushrooms are attractive reddish brown mushrooms with a smooth texture that are excellent fresh, although other fresh mushrooms may be used as substitutes if fresh *nameko* are not available.

4 cups (1 liter) Basic Dashi Stock
   (page 23) or 2 teaspoons *dashi*
   stock granules dissolved in 4 cups
   (1 liter) hot water
4 tablespoons miso
5 oz (150 g) *nameko* or other fresh
   mushrooms, rinsed
1 cake silken tofu, diced (8 oz/250 g)
4 teaspoons very finely sliced spring
   onions

1 Bring the *dashi* stock to a boil in a saucepan. Reduce the heat and add the miso, stirring to dissolve. Quickly add the mushrooms and tofu, and allow them to heat through, but do not let the soup boil. Remove from the heat.
2 Stir, then ladle the soup into four individual bowls. Sprinkle with the spring onions and serve hot.

Serves 4   Preparation time: 10 mins   Cooking time: 5 mins

Rice with Wild Vegetables and Mushrooms   Sansai Gohan

Mountain vegetables, sold as Wild Sansai Plants—usually a mixture of bracken, fern tips, *nameko* mushrooms and other mountain greens—are packed in water and sold in plastic bags or glass jars in Japanese markets. They have a wonderful "woodsy" flavor and interesting texture that transforms plain rice into a treat. Any mixture of fresh mushrooms, such as shiitake, *nameko* and porcini, works well in this recipe.

1½ cups (300 g) uncooked Japanese
   rice
2½ cups (625 ml) water
1 tablespoon sake
1 tablespoon Japanese soy sauce
1 packet mountain vegetables
7 oz (200 g) mixed fresh mushrooms
3 pieces fried tofu slices (*aburage*)
   (1 oz/30 g)
Kinome leaves or chopped parsley,
   to garnish

Rice Seasoning
1 teaspoon salt
1 teaspoon sake
1 teaspoon Japanese soy sauce
1 teaspoon *mirin*

1 Rinse and wash the rice gently. Place the rice and 2½ cups (625 ml) water in a deep saucepan and set aside to soak for 20 minutes.
2 Rinse, drain the mountain vegetables and place in a small bowl. Add the sake, soy sauce and mushrooms, mix well and set aside for 5 minutes.
3 Add the Rice Seasoning to the saucepan of soaking rice, together with the seasoned vegetables and stir. Cover the saucepan and bring to a boil over high heat for about 5 minutes, or until the water is almost fully absorbed, then stir. Reduce the heat and simmer gently, covered, for 15 minutes until the rice is cooked. Remove from the heat, place a towel over the rice (to absorb moisture) and cover with the lid. Set aside for 20 minutes.
4 Pour boiling water over the tofu slices to remove excess oil. Drain and pat dry with paper towels. Cut in half lengthwise, and then cut into short, narrow strips. Stir the fried tofu slices into the rice, garnish and serve hot.

Note: Mountain vegetables are available in packets of 5–6½ oz (150–200 g). Substitute 1 lb (500 g) of mixed fresh mushrooms, if desired. This dish can be made in a rice cooker.

Serves 4   Preparation time: 10 mins   Cooking time: 20 mins

Rice Parcels   Onigiri

These filled triangular packets of steamed rice are a traditional "travel food"—easily stuffed in the pocket or bag and ready to eat anytime. The choice of filling is up to the cook. This recipe makes 12 rice parcels.

1½ cups (300 g) uncooked Japanese rice
1¾ cups (440 ml) water (1 cup for soaking and ¾ cup added later)
Salt, to taste
2 sheets of *nori*, halved and cut into 12 rectangles
Pickled daikon radish, to garnish

Choice of Filling (per rice parcel)
½ teaspoon minced sour plum (*umeboshi*)
1 heaped teaspoon dried bonito flakes mixed with a little Japanese soy sauce
1 heaped teaspoon salted kelp (*shio-konbu*) strips
1 teaspoon salted salmon flakes (*shio zake*)
Small piece of smoked salmon

1 Rinse and wash the rice gently. Place the rice and 1 cup of the water in a saucepan and set aside to soak for 20 minutes. Add the remaining water to the pot and bring to a boil over high heat for 5 minutes. Reduce the heat to low, cover and simmer gently for 10 to 15 minutes, or until the rice is cooked. Remove from the heat, cover the rice with a towel and put the lid back on. Set aside for 15 minutes to cool.
2 To prepare the rice parcels, sprinkle a little salt onto the palm of one hand, then scoop about 2 tablespoons of rice on it. Flatten the rice, and make a depression in the center. Place a little of your chosen filling in the center. Mold the rice to enclose the filling and shape it into a triangle.
3 Wrap a piece of *nori* around the base of each parcel. Moisten the end of the *nori* to adhere, if necessary. Set aside on a serving platter and repeat from Step 2 until all the rice is used up. Cover with a piece of shrinkwrap to prevent the rice from drying out, until ready to consume. Serve at room temperature.

Makes 12 parcels   Preparation time: 20 mins   Cooking time: 20 mins

Miso Soup with Clams   Asari No Miso Shiru

30 littleneck clams or other baby clams (about 8 oz/250 g)
2 cups (500 ml) water
2 cups (500 ml) Basic Dashi Stock (page 23) or 1 teaspoon *dashi* stock granules dissolved in 2 cups (500 ml) hot water
3 tablespoons miso
Sprigs of *mitsuba* leaves, parsley or watercress, to garnish
Sansho powder, to taste

1 Soak the clams in cool, lightly salted water for 20 minutes, then scrub with a brush. Bring the water to a boil in a saucepan, then add the clams and cook for about 3 minutes or until the clams open. Remove from the heat. With a slotted spoon, portion the cooked clams into four soup bowls.
2 Strain and reserve the clam stock. Rinse the saucepan well, pour the clam stock, then the *dashi* stock into the saucepan and bring to a boil. Lower the heat, add the miso to the stock and stir to dissolve. Remove from the heat immediately. Stir, then ladle the soup over the clams and serve garnished with *mitsuba* leaves and a sprinkling of *sansho* powder.

Serves 4   Preparation time: 10 mins   Cooking time: 10 mins

Shrimp and Bamboo Shoots in Clear Broth   Wakatake-Ni

8 oz (250 g) precooked bamboo
   shoots, sliced or 1 fresh bamboo
   shoot
12–16 fresh small shrimp
2 teaspoons cornstarch
4 cups (1 liter) Basic Dashi Stock
   (page 23) or 2 teaspoons dashi
   stock granules dissolved in 4 cups
   (1 liter) of hot water
1 teaspoon sake
1 teaspoon Japanese soy sauce
1 teaspoon salt
1½ tablespoons dried *wakame*
   seaweed, rinsed and soaked
   to soften
Kinome, watercress or parsley,
   to garnish

1 Rinse and blanch the bamboo shoots. Set aside.
2 Peel the shrimp, discard the heads and tails. Slice each shrimp lengthwise without cutting through and remove the intestinal tract. Rinse and pat dry. Dust the shrimp with the cornstarch, transfer to a sieve and shake to dislodge excess cornstarch. Blanch the shrimp in boiling water for 20 seconds until the cornstarch sets. Then plunge into ice water for a few seconds and set aside.
3 Pour the *dashi* stock, sake, soy sauce and salt into a saucepan, add the bamboo shoots and bring to a boil. Add the shrimp and return to a boil and immediately remove from the heat. Garnish with the *kinome* and serve at the start of a meal.

Note: To prepare fresh bamboo shoots, place them in a saucepan with 4 cups (1 liter) water used to wash rice. Add 2 red finger chilies and simmer for about 2 hours or until soft. Peel the cooked bamboo shoots and keep under running water for 10 minutes. Quarter the shoots, store in the refrigerator, immersed in water. Cut as desired before use.

Serves 4   Preparation time: 15 mins   Cooking time: 20 mins

Grilled Eggplant and Shrimp with Miso Sauce   Nasu Miso-Ni

In this dish, the rather bland flavor of eggplant is transformed by a robust miso sauce.

1 lb (500 g) slender Japanese
   eggplants
2 tablespoons oil
8 fresh medium shrimp, peeled and
   deveined (optional)
12 snow peas, to garnish (optional)

Miso Sauce
3 tablespoons red miso
1 teaspoon sake
1 teaspoon *mirin*
2 teaspoons sugar
2 tablespoons water

1 Combine all the Miso Sauce ingredients in a small saucepan and gently heat on low for 3 minutes, stirring constantly until the sugar has dissolved and the alcohol has evaporated, then set aside.
2 Blanch the snow peas for 1 minute, drain and set aside to cool.
3 Blanch the shrimp until just cooked and pink, or for about 1 minute, and set aside.
4 Cut the eggplants in half lengthwise and score, making criss-cross incisions. Place the eggplants on a baking tray and brush with the oil. Grill for 7 minutes on each side, or until tender. Alternatively, bake at 400°F (200°C) for 15 minutes until tender.
5 Spread the Miso Sauce on the open face of the eggplants and grill or bake for another 2 minutes. Remove from the heat and serve the eggplant pieces garnished with the snow peas and shrimp.

Note: Instead of grilling or baking, the eggplants are usually cut into bite-sized pieces, deep-fried and drained. It is then mixed with the Miso Sauce (omit the water in this case), and serve with the snow peas and shrimp on the side.

Serves 4   Preparation time: 10 mins   Cooking time: 20 mins

Vegetables Simmered in Dashi and Sake Chikuzen-Ni

An array of vegetables simmered in *dashi* and rice wine creates this hearty stew which is surprisingly light and, at the same time, is healthy and delicious. Any combination of vegetables may be used, depending on availability and personal preference. The amount of stock called for in this recipe is sufficient for about 1½ lbs (750 g) of vegetables.

1½ lbs (750 g) combination of four or five types of root vegetables, such as daikon radish, burdock root, lotus root, carrot or pumpkin, baby potatoes or *sato-imo* potatoes and precooked bamboo shoots
2 oz (60 g) *konnyaku*, sliced and cut into bite-sized strips (optional)
4 fresh shiitake mushrooms, stems removed and discarded, caps halved
12 snow peas or sugar snap peas
5 oz (150 g) boneless chicken, cut into bite-sized strips (optional)
2 teaspoons oil
3 cups (750 ml) Basic Dashi Stock (page 23) or 1½ teaspoons *dashi* stock granules dissolved in 3 cups (750 ml) hot water
⅓ cup (85 ml) Japanese soy sauce
½ cup (125 ml) sake
2–3 tablespoons sugar

1 Peel and cut all the root vegetables into bite-sized chunks. Bring a small saucepan of lightly salted water to a boil. Boil the different types of vegetables separately for about 5 minutes each. Repeat with the *konnyaku*.
2 Scald the shiitake mushrooms and the sugar snap peas. Blanch the chicken pieces in hot water for 20 seconds. Drain, chill in ice water and drain again.
3 Heat the oil in a large frying pan, add the mushrooms, snow peas and chicken, stir briskly, remove from the heat and set aside.
4 Bring the *dashi* stock, soy, sake and sugar to a boil in a deep saucepan. Add the parboiled vegetables and mushrooms, and simmer gently for 15–20 minutes, or until all the vegetables are tender.
5 Portion the snow peas, chicken and the cooked vegetables into individual bowls. Pour the hot broth over and serve immediately.

Note: To prepare fresh bamboo shoots, place them in a saucepan with 4 cups (1 liter) water used to wash rice. Add 2 red finger chilies and simmer for about 2 hours or until soft. Peel the cooked bamboo shoots and keep under running water for 10 minutes. Quarter the shoots and store in the refrigerator, immersed in water. Cut as desired before use.

Serves 4   Preparation time: 20 mins   Cooking time: 40 mins

Fish Tempura in Clear Dashi Broth   Shirauo Fubuki Jitate

Fresh whitebait or baby fish dipped in batter is the highlight of this clear soup.

4 oz (125 g) fresh whitebait, cleaned, washed and patted dry
2 tablespoons cornstarch
Oil, for deep-frying
7 oz (200 g) daikon radish (about 3 in/ 8 cm), peeled and grated
4 cups (1 liter) Basic Dashi Stock (page 23) or 2 teaspoons *dashi* stock granules dissolved in 4 cups (1 liter) hot water
2 teaspoons Japanese soy sauce
2 teaspoons sake
¼ teaspoon salt, or more to taste
Mitsuba leaves to garnish (optional) or blanched chrysanthemum greens or spinach, to serve (optional)

Tempura Batter
1 egg yolk
2 tablespoons ice water
2 tablespoons cornstarch, sifted

1 Mix the Tempura Batter ingredients together in a bowl. Heat the oil in a wok. Shake the whitebait and cornstarch together in a plastic bag. Remove the coated whitebait and then dip into the Tempura Batter. Fry in hot oil until crisp and light golden. Drain on paper towels and set aside in a warm place.
2 Place the grated daikon in a muslin cloth, gently squeeze and discard the juice. Bring the *dashi* stock, soy sauce and sake almost to a boil in a saucepan and add the grated daikon. Turn off the heat, and season the soup with salt to taste.
3 Stir and ladle the soup into four soup bowls and add the fried fish just before serving. Topped with the sprigs of *mitsuba* or the blanched chrysanthemum greens or spinach.

Serves 4   Preparation time: 20 mins   Cooking time: 20 mins

Fish Marinated with Kelp   Konbu-Jime Matsumae Ae

Two types of dried kelp are used in this appetizer: regular dried kelp (*konbu*) is marinated with the fish for that extra hint of the sea, while salted kelp (*shio-konbu*) is mixed with the shredded fish at serving time.

7 oz (200 g) seabream or other fresh white fish fillet, skinned
½ teaspoon salt
4 strips dried kelp (*konbu*), (each 4 in/10 cm long), wiped with a damp cloth
Few sprigs *mitsuba* or watercress stems, scalded and sliced
8 small pieces (⅓ oz/10 g) salted kelp (*shio-konbu*), sliced into thin strips
1 teaspoon wasabi paste or horse-radish, to serve

1 Cut the fish into slices about ¼ in (½ cm) thick and sprinkle with salt. Lay two pieces of the kelp on a plate and place the slices of fish on it. Top with the remaining kelp to make a "sandwich." Cover with a lid and a weight to press, and refrigerate for 2 days, turning the kelp–fish sandwich over after the first day.
2 When the fish is ready for serving, slice the *mitsuba* into short lengths, then scald and drain. Slice the salted kelp into thin strips. Unwrap the chilled fish and discard the kelp. Slice the fish into thin strips and mix with the *mitsuba* and salted kelp. Serve on small plates with wasabi paste on the side.

Serves 4   Preparation time: 15 mins + 2 days to marinate   Cooking time: 5 mins

Golden Cuttlefish   Ika Kimi Yaki

The egg glaze used in this recipe gives grilled cuttlefish an attractive golden coating. It helps to seal and keep the meat moist. Golden Cuttlefish and Crispy Seasoned Whitebait are served together with Shrimp and Bamboo Shoots in Clear Broth (page 44) as a starter during special occasions. The pairing of the succulent cuttlefish and the crisp salty-sweet whitebait (see recipe below) creates a nice balance of texture and taste. This dish is best made with octopus as it has the thickest and firmest flesh of all types of cuttlefish.

3 egg yolks
8 oz (250 g) fresh octopus flesh,
   cuttlefish flesh or firm white fish fillet
¼ teaspoon salt
Small pastry brush

1 Beat the egg yolks lightly in a bowl and set aside.
2 Using a sharp knife, lightly score to mark parallel lines ¼ in (½ cm) wide on the cuttlefish flesh. Sprinkle with salt, then thread the cuttlefish flesh onto two or more skewers to prevent it from curling during the cooking process.
3 Set the broiler at moderate heat. Grill the cuttlefish very quickly for 2 minutes on each side. Brush the egg glaze on the cuttlefish and continue to grill until the egg glaze sets. Turn the cuttlefish over and brush again. Repeat three to four times, until the glaze is an even, golden yellow—this will take about 5 minutes. Make sure not to overcook the meat or the texture of the cuttlefish will be rubbery. Remove the skewers and slice the grilled cuttlefish through the scored lines and serve.

Note: If using fish fillet, sprinkle with salt and cut into four pieces then skewer. Heat the grill and brush it with a little oil to prevent the fish from sticking to the grill pan, then follow the recipe from Step 3.

Serves 4   Preparation time: 7 mins   Cooking time: 10 mins

Crispy Seasoned Whitebait   Chirimenjako

This recipe for whitebait coated with a crispy soy-and-sugar glaze makes a wonderful snack or appetizer on its own, and it washes well with beer, sake or cocktails.

5 oz (150 g) dried whitebait or small
   dried anchovies
2 tablespoons *mirin*
1 tablespoon Japanese soy sauce
3 tablespoons sugar
2 tablespoons water
Seven-spice chili powder (*shichimi*),
   to taste (optional)
White sesame seeds, to garnish
   (optional)

1 Place the dried whitebait in a frying pan and dry-fry over medium-high heat for 10 minutes, shaking the pan frequently or stirring constantly until light brown and fragrant. Remove from the heat and set the fish aside in a small plate. If using fish more than 1½ in (4 cm) long, remove the heads and bones.
2 Combine the *mirin*, soy sauce, sugar and water in a small saucepan, bring to a boil, then lower the heat and simmer until the liquid is reduced by half and has a thick syrupy consistency. Add the whitebait and stir to coat well with the sugar glaze.
3 Sprinkle with the seven-spice chili powder and white sesame seeds and serve together with Golden Cuttlefish (see above).

Serves 4   Preparation time: 5 mins   Cooking time: 10 mins

Duck or Chicken Dumplings and Tofu in Clear Broth

Kamo Tsumire

An unusual combination of duck meat with *yamato* potato makes for very soft and light meatballs in this delicate and healthy dish reminiscent of *matzo* balls.

4 cups (1 liter) Basic Dashi Stock
  (page 23) or 2 teaspoons *dashi*
  stock granules dissolved in 4 cups
  (1 liter) hot water
¼ teaspoon salt, or more to taste
2 teaspoons Japanese soy sauce
2 teaspoons sake
1 cake (8 oz/250 g) silken tofu, sliced
  into pieces
Spring onion, green part only, thinly
  sliced, to garnish

Duck or Chicken Dumplings
1 cup (8 oz/250 g) ground duck
  breast or chicken breast
½ cup (60 g) *yamato* potato, peeled
  and finely grated
1 teaspoon cornstarch
2 teaspoons miso
½ teaspoon finely grated young
  ginger
1 egg, lightly beaten

1 Pour the *dashi* stock into a saucepan, bring to a boil and add the salt, soy sauce and sake. Reduce the heat and keep warm.

2 To make the dumplings, combine all the ingredients in a bowl and mix well. Wet one hand, scoop a tablespoon of the mixture onto the wet palm and shape into a patty. Drop the dumplings gently into the simmering broth and cook for 5 minutes. Repeat until the mixture is used up. Remove the cooked dumplings with a slotted spoon and portion into individual serving bowls. Set aside in a warm place.

3 Using a small mesh basket with a long handle, lower the tofu into the broth to heat through. Add the tofu to the bowls of dumplings. Ladle the broth into the bowls. Garnish with the sliced spring onion and serve at the start of a meal.

Note: *Yamato* potato is a starchy root and, when grated, has a viscous, almost gluey texture. If it is not available, add 2 more teaspoons of cornstarch or ½ cup mashed silken tofu.

Serves 4   Preparation time: 20 mins   Cooking time: 10 mins

Crispy Stuffed Lotus Root Karashi Renkon

1 fresh lotus root (7 oz/200 g)
Oil, for deep-frying

Egg Filling
3 hard-boiled egg yolks
2 tablespoons white miso
1 teaspoon prepared Japanese
  mustard paste
½ teaspoon caster sugar
½ teaspoon salt
1 heaped tablespoon cornstarch

Batter
2 egg yolks
4 tablespoons ice water
1 heaped tablespoon cornstarch

1 Prepare the Egg Filling by mashing the egg yolks, then mixing them well with the miso, mustard, sugar and salt.

2 Scrub and peel the lotus root. Cover with water in a saucepan and boil for 5 minutes. Drain and slice off the ends. Cut the lotus root into three equal sections, and chill for 15 minutes in the refrigerator.

3 Dust the lotus root sections with a bit of cornstarch, making sure it coats the sides of the holes. Stuff the lotus root holes with the Egg Filling, pressing it in with the blunt end of a chopstick until compact.

4 Prepare the batter by mixing the egg yolks and the water, then add the cornstarch and stir briefly. The batter should be a little lumpy.

5 Heat the oil in a wok. Coat the stuffed lotus root with the batter and deep-fry in hot oil. Drain on paper towels and cut each section into ½-in (1-cm) thick slices. Serve immediately with a sprinkling of salt.

Serves 4   Preparation time: 30 mins   Cooking time: 5 mins

Cold Soba Noodles with Assorted Toppings

Soba noodles made from buckwheat flour are eaten both cold and hot in Japan. These chilled noodles are wonderful in summertime, and the toppings can be varied according to the ingredients on hand.

1 packet dried soba noodles or buckwheat pasta (about 7 oz/200 g)
2 cups (500 ml) Cold Soba Dashi Broth (page 23)

Simmered Shiitake Mushrooms
12 dried Chinese black mushrooms, rinsed and soaked in ¾ cup (185 ml) water
  for 10 minutes to soften, stems discarded and soaking liquid reserved, or
  20 fresh shiitake mushrooms, stems discarded, soaked in ½ cup (125 ml) water
1½ teaspoons sugar
1½ teaspoons Japanese soy sauce

Tempura Fritters
1 egg yolk
4 tablespoons ice water
4 tablespoons cornstarch
½ burdock root (about 3½ oz/100 g), peeled and grated
1 small carrot, peeled and grated
1 onion, very thinly sliced
1 tablespoon minced *mitsuba* or parsley leaves
Oil, for deep-frying

Toppings
4 teaspoons wasabi paste
4 heaped tablespoons finely shredded *nori*
2 eggs, lightly beaten, fried as a thin omelet, then very thinly sliced
8 *shiso* leaves, very thinly sliced
2 spring onions, white part only, finely sliced into shreds
1¼ oz (40 g) salmon or tuna, poached and flaked
  or ¾ oz (20 g) salted salmon flakes (*shio zake*)
2 tablespoons *konbu tsukudani* (kelp simmered in soy sauce, *mirin* and sugar)

1 Boil the noodles in plenty of lightly salted water for 4 to 5 minutes, uncovered, drain and chill in cold water. Drain again and refrigerate. Simmer the Cold Soba Dashi Broth (page 23) over medium-high heat for 10 minutes and set aside.
2 To cook the Simmered Shiitake Mushrooms, combine all the ingredients in a saucepan and bring to a boil. Reduce the heat and simmer for 10 minutes and set aside to cool. Drain and slice the mushroom caps very finely.
3 Prepare the tempura batter by mixing the egg yolk, ice water and cornstarch in a bowl and stir briskly. The batter should be slightly lumpy. Heat the oil in a frying pan until very hot. Combine and mix the tempura vegetables in a bowl. Take a small handful of the vegetables and dip it in the batter, remove with a slotted spoon. Gently slide the vegetables into the hot oil and deep-fry until light golden brown. Drain on paper towels and set aside.
4 When serving, arrange small portions (enough for two mouthfuls) of the noodles in small bowls. Pour a little broth over the noodles and add the preferred combination of Toppings. Repeat, varying the combination of Toppings.

Serves 4   Preparation time: 30 mins   Cooking time: 40 mins

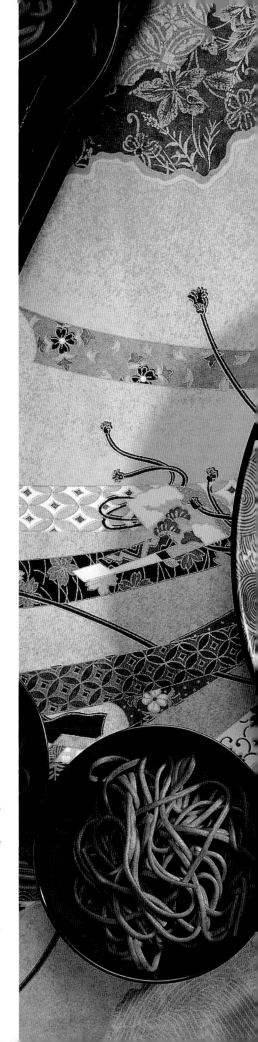

Hot Soba Noodle Soup with Tempura Tempura Soba

7 oz (200 g) soba noodles or buckwheat pasta
12 cups (3 liters) water
1 teaspoon salt
Finely sliced spring onions, to garnish
Seven-spice chili powder (shichimi),
  to serve

Hot Soba Dashi Broth
4 cups (1 liter) Basic Dashi Stock
  (page 23) or 2 teaspoons dashi
  stock granules dissolved in 4 cups
  (1 liter) hot water
3 tablespoons Japanese soy sauce
1 tablespoon mirin

Tempura Batter
1 egg yolk
1 cup (250 ml) ice water
1 cup (150 g) cornstarch

Tempura
8 fresh medium shrimp
Cornstarch, for dusting
4 fresh shiitake mushrooms, stems
  discarded, caps left whole
4 shiso leaves
Oil, for deep-frying

1 In an uncovered saucepan, boil the noodles in plenty of lightly salted water for 4 to 5 minutes, drain and chill in cold water, then drain again. Set aside.
2 To make the Hot Soba Dashi Broth, place all the ingredients into a saucepan, bring to a boil and immediately remove from the heat. Set aside in a warm place.
3 Make the Tempura Batter by mixing the egg yolk, ice water and cornstarch in a bowl and stir briskly. The batter should be slightly lumpy.
4 To prepare the Tempura, peel the shrimp, discard the heads and keep the tails intact. Slit the back of each shrimp and devein. Make several small incisions crosswise along the underside of the shrimp to prevent it from curling during the frying process.
5 Preheat the oil in a wok or saucepan until very hot. Dust each shrimp with the cornstarch, shake off any excess, then dip in the Tempura Batter and deep-fry in very hot oil for 1–2 minutes until light golden. Drain on paper towels. Dip the shiitake mushrooms and shiso leaves in the batter and deep-fry. Drain on paper towels.
6 Divide the soba noodles into four bowls and ladle the broth over the noodles. Top with 2 shrimp, mushroom and shiso leaf in each bowl, and garnish with the spring onions and a sprinkling of seven-spice chili powder.

Note: Substitute shrimp with small fish such as whiting, fresh whitebait or vegetables such as pumpkin, sweet potatoes and eggplants.

Serves 4   Preparation time: 30 mins   Cooking time: 45 mins

Rice with Green Tea and Wasabi Ochazuke

This is a delightful and unusual snack or lunch dish—steamed rice with a light green tea or dashi broth and various toppings—and is very easy to prepare.

2½–3 cups (450 g) cooked rice
4 heaped tablespoons salted salmon
  flakes (shio zake)
3 cups (750 ml) hot Japanese green
  tea, prepared from ¾ teaspoon
  matcha green tea powder mixed
  with 3 cups (750 ml) boiling water
Shredded nori, to garnish
Shiso leaves or spring onions, thinly
  sliced, to garnish
2 teaspoons wasabi paste, to serve

1 Divide the rice among four rice bowls. Top each bowl with 1 tablespoon salmon flakes.
2 Make the tea just before serving. Pour in enough hot green tea or dashi stock to cover the rice in each bowl. Garnish with the nori and shiso leaves or spring onions. Serve each portion with ½ teaspoon of the wasabi paste and pickles on the side.

Note: Substitute the green tea with 4 cups (1 liter) Basic Dashi Stock (page 23) or 2 teaspoons dashi stock granules dissolved in 4 cups (1 liter) of hot water.

Serves 4   Preparation time: 15 mins

Assorted Sashimi Sashimi Moriawase

A wide variety of seafood is enjoyed raw as sashimi in Japan, each one sliced in different ways depending upon the texture of the particular ingredient. Sashimi is served with a variety of garnishes, condiments and dipping sauces. You may decide to serve just one or two types of fish, or a range of seafood, but whatever you choose, be absolutely certain that it is fresh.

8 fresh medium shrimp
¼ lb (125 g) freshly shucked scallops
½ teaspoon oil
5 oz (150 g) fresh tuna fillet
5 oz (150 g) fresh salmon fillet
5 oz (150 g) fresh mackerel or snapper fillet
8 oz (250 g) daikon radish (about 4 in/10 cm), grated into long thin shreds
4 *shiso* leaves
4 teaspoons wasabi paste

Sashimi Soy Dip
3 tablespoons sake
½ cup (125 ml) Japanese soy sauce
2 tablespoons *tamari* soy sauce or *mirin*
½ cup (5 g) dried bonito flakes
1 small strip dried kelp (*konbu*), wiped with a damp cloth (optional)

1 To make the Sashimi Soy Dip, place all the ingredients in a small saucepan and simmer on medium-low heat for 5 minutes. Remove from the heat, allow to cool, strain and discard solids. Set aside.
2 Peel and clean the shrimp, but leave the head and tail on for a more authentic appearance. Clean and dry the scallops. Heat the oil in a pan until moderately hot and sear the scallops for 30 seconds on each side. Remove from the heat and set aside.
3 Slice the tuna and salmon fillets on the diagonal into strips about ½ in (1 cm) wide and 1½ in (3 cm) long. The mackerel or snapper can either be sliced paper-thin or cut into decorative shapes.
4 Arrange the shrimp, scallops and cut fish on a serving platter. Garnish with the daikon, *shiso* leaves and wasabi paste, and serve with small bowls of Sashimi Soy Dip.

Note: The Sashimi Soy Dip can be stored for up to a year if kept refrigerated in an airtight jar.

Serves 4   Preparation time: 30 mins   Cooking time: 1 min

Rolled Sushi   Hosomaki

Three different fillings are used in this recipe for *nori*-wrapped rolls of vinegared rice—tuna, cucumber and pickled daikon—the last is available in plastic packets in Japanese stores. Other fillings may also be used—for example carrot, crabstick and omelet strips.

2 cups (400 g) cooked Sushi Rice (page 25)
3 sheets toasted nori, each about 8 x 7 in (20 x 18 cm), halved
2 teaspoons wasabi paste
Pickled young ginger slices, to serve
Sashimi Soy Dip (page 25), to serve

Fillings
1 Japanese cucumber
5 oz (150 g) pickled daikon radish
7 oz (200 g) fresh tuna

Makes 6 rolls
Preparation time: 20 mins

1 Follow the instructions on page 25 to make the Sushi Rice. While the rice is cooking, cut the cucumbers into quarters lengthwise. Remove seeds from the cucumbers, if any. Slice the pickled daikon into long, thin strips. Cut the tuna into long strips. Set the Fillings aside.
2 Place a halved *nori* sheet on a bamboo rolling mat with the shiny side down. Spread 1/3 cup (70 g) of the cooked Sushi Rice evenly on the *nori* sheet, leaving a border of about 1/2 in (1 cm) exposed along the top edge. Dab a little wasabi along the center of the rice. Place 2 strips of the cucumber across the center of the wasabi.
3 To roll, hold the edge of the mat nearest to you with one hand, press the cucumber with the other hand to hold it in place, and roll the mat over the rice. Lift the top of the mat and complete the roll, squeezing gently along the length of the roll. Unroll the mat, and press to seal. Roll the sushi in the mat again. Slice the roll in half, and cut both rolls twice to give six uniform pieces. Repeat with the remaining cucumber, daikon radish and tuna fillings. Serve with the pickled ginger and Sashimi Soy Dip on the side.

Sushi Rice with Assorted Toppings   Chirashi-Zushi

Chirashi means "to scatter." In this dish, sushi rice, topped with seafood and eggs, is served in a bowl. Vegetables or cooked meat can be added for variety. *Chirashi-zushi* is eaten as a one-bowl meal, or served in a large bowl to be shared among a group of people.

2–3 cups (400–600 g) cooked Sushi Rice (page 25)
1 tablespoon dried whitebait or silverfish, dry-fried for about 5–10 minutes in a pan until crisp (optional)
3 eggs, lightly beaten and fried as an omelet, then very thinly sliced
8 medium shrimp, cooked, peeled, deveined, sliced butterfly style
3 oz (90 g) fresh tuna, cut into strips
1 piece (2 oz/60 g) squid, blanched lightly and cut into strips
1 strip (3 oz/90 g) barbequed eel (optional)
Nori, thinly shredded, to garnish
Pickled young ginger slices, to serve
Sashimi Soy Dip (page 25) or Japanese soy sauce, to serve
Wasabi paste, to serve

Shrimp Flakes
5 oz (150 g) small fresh shrimp, peeled and deveined
1 egg yolk
2–3 teaspoons sugar
1/2 teaspoon salt

1 Follow the instructions on page 25 to make the Sushi Rice (make 1 1/2 portions for this recipe as a main course).
2 Prepare the Shrimp Flakes by simmering the shrimp in a saucepan with a little salted water until the shrimp change color. Drain, cool and blend in a food processor. Place the ground shrimp into a bowl and add the egg yolk, sugar and salt and mix well. Place the mixture in a pan and dry-fry over very low heat, stirring constantly, for about 10 minutes or until almost dry and flaky. Transfer to a dry plate and set aside. This can be kept refrigerated for a week.
3 Mix the Sushi Rice with the dried whitebait (if using) in a wide wooden bowl. With the back of a spoon, pack the rice into four lacquer bowls or boxes and level the surface.
4 Scatter the sliced omelet over the rice and top with the shrimp, tuna, squid and eel. Garnish with the shredded *nori* and Shrimp Flakes, and serve with pickled ginger, Sashimi Soy Dip and wasabi paste on the side.

Note: Silverfish are tiny fish sold cured or dried in packets, and barbequed eel is available either canned or in vacuum packs. Other non-traditional ingredients such as barbequed pork or beef, smoked oysters or salmon may also be used. Substitute Shrimp Flakes with prepared salted salmon flakes (*shio zake*), which are available in Japanese specialty stores, sold in plastic packets or bottled.

Serves 4   Preparation time: 40 mins   Cooking time: 40 mins

Mixed Rolled Sushi   Norimaki

3 cups (600 g) cooked Sushi Rice (page 25)
1 Japanese cucumber, quartered
6–8 fresh medium shrimp, cooked, peeled and halved lengthwise (optional)
4 sheets toasted *nori,* each about 8 x 7 in (20 x 18 cm)
4 heaped tablespoons Shrimp Flakes (page 61)
  or salted salmon flakes (*shio zake*)
1 portion Simmered Shiitake Mushrooms (page 54)
Pickled young ginger slices, to serve
Sashimi Soy Dip (page 25) or Japanese soy sauce, to serve

Japanese Omelet
3 eggs
4 tablespoons Basic Dashi Stock (page 23) or ¼ teaspoon *dashi* stock
  granules dissolved in 4 tablespoons hot water
2 tablespoons *mirin*
1½ teaspoons sugar
¼ teaspoon salt
Oil, for greasing

1 Prepare the Sushi Rice by following the instructions on page 25. Repeat with half the amounts specified in the recipe, to make 1½ portions of Sushi Rice in total. Cover and set aside.
2 Prepare the Japanese Omelet by combining all the ingredients in a bowl, stirring gently until the sugar has dissolved. Heat a small omelet pan over medium heat and brush lightly with the oil. Lower the heat. Pour a little egg mixture (enough to make a thin omelet) slowly into the pan, swirling the pan for the mixture to spread evenly. Use a spatula or chopstick to break up any bubbles that may form. When the egg is about to set, fold two sides of the omelet toward the center, overlapping each other. Remove and set the omelet onto a dry plate. Cook a second omelet. When the egg is set at the bottom and still moist on top, place the first omelet in the center of the pan and fold the two sides over. Remove and set aside on the dry plate again. Repeat with the remaining egg mixture until it is all used up. Set the omelet onto a bamboo mat or kitchen towel, roll and squeeze gently to remove moisture. Unroll and flatten the omelet slightly. Slice the omelet lengthwise into long rectangular strips.
3 Place a *nori* sheet on a bamboo mat and spread a quarter portion of the Sushi Rice on the *nori,* leaving ½ in (1 cm) of the *nori* exposed along the top. Sprinkle 1 tablespoon of the Shrimp Flakes along the center of the rice. Lay a quarter of the seasoned mushrooms over it. Place a quarter of the omelet strips, cucumber and shrimp along the center of the rice.
4 First, roll the mat once over the ingredients, pressing the ingredients in to keep the roll firm. Lift the mat and complete the roll, pressing the mat firmly all around. Unroll the mat, and use your finger to ensure that the roll is sealed. Roll the sushi rice again, using fingers to press the roll into a circle. Remove and slice each roll in half, and cut each half into four pieces. Repeat with the remaining fillings to make another three rolls. Serve with the pickled ginger and Sashimi Soy Dip on the side.

Makes 4 rolls   Preparation time: 50 mins   Cooking time: 40 mins

Beef Sushi   Gyu-Nigiri

Well-marbled beef is normally used for this dish, which is the Japanese equivalent of Italian *carpaccio*. If you prefer, the beef may be quickly seared on the outside before slicing, and may also be marinated beforehand with Teriyaki Sauce (page 24) and barbequed.

1 cup (150 g) cooked Sushi Rice
  (page 25)
5 oz (150 g) prime marbled beef
  sirloin, very thinly sliced
1 teaspoon crushed garlic
Shiso flowers or alternative garnish
Benitade or alfalfa sprouts, to garnish
4 tablespoons pickled young ginger
  slices, to serve
Ponzu Dipping Sauce (page 24), to
  serve or Sashimi Soy Dip (page 25),
  to serve

1 Make the Sushi Rice by preparing half of the amounts specified in the recipe on page 25. While the rice is cooking, cut the beef into thin slices about 2½ in (6 cm) long by ¾ in (2 cm) wide by ¼ in (3 cm) thick. Hold a beef slice in one hand and, using a small spoon, spread a little of the crushed garlic on it. Moisten your other hand and pinch a heaped tablespoonful of the Sushi Rice and form a small cylinder in the palm of your hand. Lay the rice onto the seasoned side of the beef and press lightly, for the beef to adhere to the rice.

2 Arrange on a platter and garnish with the *shiso* flowers, *benitade* or alfalfa sprouts. Serve with the pickled ginger and Ponzu Dipping Sauce.

Serves 4   Preparation time: 20 mins   Cooking time: 40 mins

Fresh Shellfish Sashimi   Aka-Gai Sashimi

Cockles, also known as ark shell, can reach a diameter of 5 in (12 cm). The best quality cockles are harvested in spring, and only the freshest ones are eaten raw. Expert sashimi chefs have a beautiful way of slicing fresh shellfish and a unique method of tenderizing the meat in preparation for a delightfully mouth-watering sashimi treat—by flinging the meat onto the cutting board several times!

8–12 fresh cockles, giant clams or
  scallops, in the shell
7 oz (200 g) daikon radish (about 3 in/
  8 cm), cut into shreds
Ohba or *shiso* leaves, to garnish
Shiso flowers or alternative garnish
Benitade or alfalfa sprouts, to garnish
Wasabi paste, to serve
Sashimi Soy Dip (page 25), to serve

1 Open the shellfish by inserting a knife along the back of the shells and cutting the muscles. Remove the meat, discarding the hard parts and entrails. Slit the cockles or clams down the center, without cutting through, and open to form a butterfly shape. Cut several shallow slits on the outside of the cockle meat. Cut in half and tenderize if needed.

2 Arrange the shellfish on the shredded daikon or on the leaves, and garnish with the *shiso* flowers and *benitade*. Serve with the wasabi paste and dip.

Note: *Ohba* leaves make an elegant garnish for this dish. They are commonly referred to as Japanese basil or mint, and their fragrance resembles a combination of cumin, cilantro and parsley with a hint of cinnamon. The leaves have a stronger flavor than *shiso* leaves, and are sometimes used to wrap sushi. They are sold in plastic packets and are available in some Asian food stores.

Serves 4   Preparation time: 30 mins

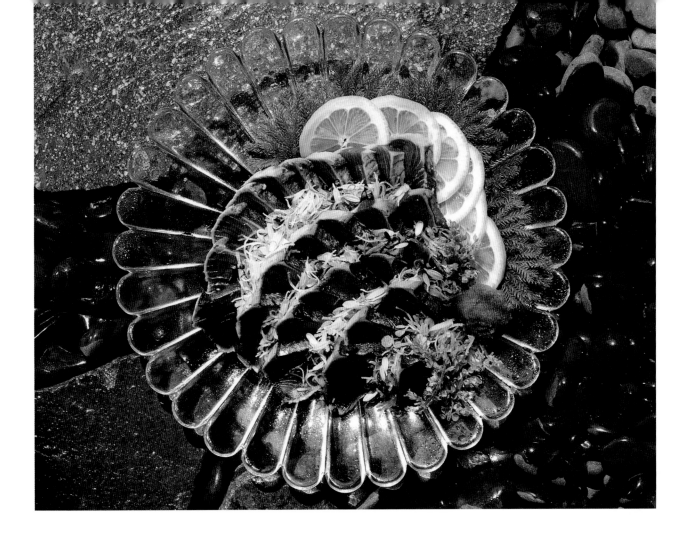

Seared Tataki Bonito with Tangy Dressing Katsuo Tataki

Tataki means "to pound," and refers to a method in which seasoned meat is lightly beaten with a knife to enhance its flavor. Lightly seared fish is marinated with tangy seasonings in this refreshing chilled dish—a perfect starter for the hot summer months.

Oil, to grease pan
12 oz (350 g) fresh bonito fillet, skin left on, tuna or horse mackerel
1/3 cup (30 g) spring onions, thinly sliced into shreds
1 in (2½ cm) young ginger, finely shredded
1–2 cloves garlic, minced
½ lemon, thinly sliced
1/3 cup (85 ml) Ponzu Dipping Sauce (page 24)
4 oz (125 g) daikon radish (about 2 in/ 5 cm), sliced into long thin strips
Chrysanthemum flowers, to garnish
1 heaped tablespoon finely grated daikon mixed with ¼ teaspoon seven-spice chili powder (*shichimi*) or ground red pepper, to serve

1 Heat a lightly greased frying pan. Sear the fish until the outside of the flesh just turns white. Using a pair of chopsticks, turn and sear the other side, then immediately chill in the refrigerator or freeze to stop the fish from cooking further.

2 Once the fish has cooled, wipe away any moisture and marinate the whole fillet in half of the spring onions, ginger, garlic, lemon and half of the Ponzu Dipping Sauce. Pat the fish with the side of a knife to help the sauce penetrate. Chill in the refrigerator for a minimum of 10 minutes. Cut the marinated fish into small slices ½-in (1-cm) thick.

3 Arrange the fish and lemon slices on a bed of daikon strips. Sprinkle the remaining sliced spring onions, ginger, garlic and the edible flowers over the fish. Serve chilled or at room temperature with the remaining Ponzu Dipping Sauce in a small bowl and seasoned grated daikon on the side.

Serves 4   Preparation time: 10 mins   Cooking time: 5 mins

Pressed Mackerel Sushi Battera Sushi

This is a quick and easy way of making sushi by pressing the rice and fish into a box then turning it out and slicing it, rather than shaping it with the hand. In Japan, marinated mackerel is used. However, fresh or pickled herring or smoked salmon works very well.

2 cups cooked Sushi Rice (page 25)
10 oz (300 g) fresh mackerel or
  herring fillets, skins intact
¾ teaspoon salt
2 tablespoons caster sugar
¾ cup (185 ml) rice vinegar
1–2 teaspoons wasabi paste
1 tablespoon vinegar, mixed in ¼ cup
  (60 ml) water
1 teaspoon white sesame seeds
Japanese soy sauce, to serve
Pickled young ginger slices, to serve
1 cake pan or non-reactive plastic
  box (about 7 x 5 in/18 x 12 cm) or
  oshiwaku (wooden sushi pressing
  box with cover)

Makes 14 pieces   Preparation time:
20 mins + 2 hours refrigeration and
1 hour to marinate

1 Make the Sushi Rice by following the recipe on page 25. While the rice is cooking, remove any small bones from the mackerel or herring fillets. Sprinkle the fish lightly with the salt and refrigerate for at least 2 hours.
2 Dissolve the sugar in the vinegar. Rinse the salt off the fish and immerse in the sweetened vinegar. Marinate for 1 hour, then remove the fish and gently pull off the thin membrane covering the skin.
3 Line the bottom of a cake pan with wax paper or a damp cotton cloth. Lay the fillets in the box, skin side down. Slice the fillets, if necessary, to cover the base of the box. Spread the wasabi paste over the fish.
4 Moisten your fingers with a little diluted vinegar and spread half the Sushi Rice over the fish. Sprinkle the sesame seeds and add the remaining rice and spread evenly in the cake pan. To compress the rice, lay a piece of shrinkwrap over it, then place a piece of cardboard on top and press firmly. You may also use a smaller box with a flat base that fits into the cake pan to compress the rice. Set aside in a cool place until ready to serve.
5 Turn the rice and fish out onto a cutting board. Carefully wet a sharp knife with the diluted vinegar and slice the sushi into small rectangles using long sawing motions. Serve with dipping bowls of soy sauce and pickled ginger.

Shrimp Simmered in Sake   Ebi-Ni

12–16 fresh large shrimp

16 snow peas or 2 cups sliced spinach or Chinese cabbage, to serve

1 cup (250 ml) Basic Dashi Stock (page 23) or ½ teaspoon *dashi* stock granules dissolved in 1 cup (250 ml) hot water

⅔ cup (150 ml) sake

1 teaspoon sugar

3 teaspoons Japanese soy sauce

1 in (2½ cm) young ginger, bruised

1 Trim the whiskers and legs of each shrimp. Using a small knife, make a small incision along the mid-section in the back of the shrimp and devein by gently pulling out the intestinal tract.

2 Blanch the vegetables in lightly salted water for 2 minutes. Drain and portion into individual serving platters and set aside.

3 Place the shrimp in a pan with the *dashi* stock, sake, sugar, soy sauce and ginger. Cook over high heat for 3 to 4 minutes, or until the shrimp turns pink. Remove the shrimp from the heat. Serve the warm broth on the side if desired.

4 Peel the shrimp, keeping the heads and tails intact. Serve immediately on the bed of greens.

Serves 4   Preparation time: 10 mins   Cooking time: 5 mins

Steamed Fish with Noodles in Clear Broth   Banshu-Mushi

7 oz (200 g) red snapper, tile fish or redfish

½ teaspoon salt

4 oz (125 g) dried fine wheat noodles (*somen*) or angel hair pasta

3½ oz (100 g) *shimeji* mushrooms

1 heaped tablespoon grated daikon, mixed with ¼ teaspoon ground red pepper

2 spring onions, white part only, very thinly sliced

Clear Broth

1 cup (250 ml) Basic Dashi Stock (page 23) or ½ teaspoon *dashi* stock granules dissolved in 1 cup (250 ml) hot water

1 tablespoon sake

1 tablespoon *mirin*

½ teaspoon Japanese soy sauce

Salt, to taste

1 To make the Clear Broth, bring all the ingredients to a boil in a saucepan over medium-high heat. Remove from the heat and set aside in a warm place.

2 Sprinkle the fish with salt, then slice into four pieces. Place on a heat-proof dish and steam for 5 minutes. Remove and set aside.

3 Cook the noodles in lightly salted boiling water, until soft. Drain and immediately rinse under cold water and drain again.

4 Divide the noodles into four individual serving bowls. Place a piece of fish and portion the *shimeji* mushrooms on the noodles in each bowl. Return to the steamer. Steam the fish again over rapidly boiling water for 5 minutes.

5 Remove the bowls from the steamer and pour in the Clear Broth. Serve with grated daikon on the side and garnish with the spring onions.

Serves 4   Preparation time: 15 mins   Cooking time: 15 mins

Simmered Fish in a Light Daikon Broth

7 oz (200 g) daikon radish (about
  3 in/8 cm)
1 strip dried kelp (konbu) (4 in/10 cm)
3 cups (375 liter) water
1/3 cup (85 ml) sake
2 tablespoons mirin
1 tablespoon Japanese soy sauce
Salt, to taste (optional)
8 oz (250 g) snapper or salmon fillet,
  sliced into 8 pieces
Cooked lobster meat or shrimp,
  sliced, to garnish (optional)
Spring onion, thinly sliced, to garnish

1 Peel and slice the daikon into four sections. Place the daikon, konbu and water in a saucepan and simmer over low heat for 45 minutes or until the daikon is tender. Discard the solids or reserve the daikon to serve later if desired.
2 Add the sake, mirin and soy sauce to the broth and continue to simmer for another 10 minutes.
3 Add the fish and simmer for another 3 to 4 minutes, or until cooked. Add a pinch of salt to taste. Portion the fish into four bowls, and top with the lobster meat or shrimp, if using. Ladle the hot broth and serve immediately, garnished with the spring onion.

Serves 4   Preparation time: 15 mins   Cooking time: 1 hour

Steamed Seabass with Vegetables   Shiba-Mushi

10 oz (300 g) seabass, grouper, or
  cod or baramundi fillets, cut into
  4 pieces
1/2 teaspoon salt
2 tablespoons sake
8 oz (250 g) enokitake mushrooms
4 oz (125 g) shimeji mushrooms
1/2 cup (125 ml) Basic Dashi Stock
  (page 23) or 1/4 teaspoon dashi
  stock granules dissolved in 1/2 cup
  (125 ml) hot water
10 thin asparagus spears (2 oz/60 g),
  cut into lengths
1 small carrot, cut into strips
1 spring onion, cut into lengths,
  to garnish

Broth
1 cup (250 ml) Basic Dashi Stock
  (page 23) or 1/2 teaspoon dashi
  stock granules dissolved in 1 cup
  (250 ml) hot water
2 tablespoons mirin
1 tablespoon Japanese soy sauce
1 teaspoon salt

1 To make the Broth, combine all the ingredients in a saucepan and bring almost to a boil, then turn off the heat. Cover and set aside.
2 Place the fish in a large shallow bowl, rub with the salt and allow to sit for 20 minutes. Sprinkle the sake over the fish and steam for 5 minutes and set aside.
3 Discard the hard ends of the stems of the enokitake mushrooms. Discard the stems of the shimeji mushrooms and halve crosswise. Pour the dashi stock into another saucepan and simmer the mushrooms for 1–2 minutes. Drain and set aside. Blanch the asparagus and carrots in lightly salted water. Drain and set aside.
4 Place the steamed seabass into four serving bowls and arrange the vegetables and mushrooms on top. Ladle the hot Broth over the fish. Garnish with the spring onion, and serve immediately.

Serves 4   Preparation time: 30 mins   Cooking time: 10 mins

Tuna and Daikon Simmered in Sake and Soy Buri No Nitsuke

This sweet and robustly flavored stew is usually made with the head of a yellowtail tuna. It is simmered for at least an hour for the optimum fusion of wine, sugar and soy with the seafood. The length of the stewing time depends on the type of fish available, and if you are using fillets or whole fish with bones. Catfish, carp, grouper, seabream or any kind of rock fish is ideal for stewing.

1 lb (500 g) yellowtail tuna or other fresh, firm fish
8 oz (250 g) daikon radish (about 4 in/10 cm), peeled and sliced into 4 thick sections
1½ cups (375 ml) rice washing water or regular water
5 cups (1¼ liters) water
2 cups (500 ml) sake
1 in (2½ cm) young ginger, grated
1–2 tablespoons sugar
4 tablespoons Japanese dark soy sauce or 2 tablespoons *tamari* and 2 tablespoons Japanese soy sauce
Kinome or watercress, to garnish

1 Cut the fish into chunks of four or eight pieces. Blanch the fish in boiling water for 10 to 20 seconds. Drain and set aside. Boil the sliced daikon for 15 minutes in water in which rice has been washed. (This water helps the daikon remain white.) Drain and chill in ice water and drain again.
2 Pour the water and sake into a large pot. Add the fish, cooked daikon and grated ginger. Bring to a boil over high heat and simmer for 5 minutes, skimming the foam from the surface regularly, then add the sugar and reduce the heat to low. Simmer uncovered for 20 to 30 minutes until the liquid has reduced by half. Add the soy sauce and continue simmering, uncovered, for another 10 to 20 minutes, by which time the liquid will have reduced to about half.
3 Place the fish and daikon in a large bowl, topped with *kinome* or watercress to garnish. Serve hot with steamed rice and pickles on the side.

Serves 4–6   Preparation time: 15 mins   Cooking time: 1 hour

Steamed Egg Custard Cups with Shrimp, Chicken and Mushrooms Chawan-Mushi

This traditional silky smooth egg custard dish may be served as an appetizer or main course. Blanched vegetables such as asparagus, carrots and spinach may be substituted for the chicken and shrimp. In Japan, *chawan-mushi* is prepared and served in tall, dainty teacups and eaten with a bamboo spoon.

3 oz (90 g) chicken breast, thinly sliced
5 teaspoons Japanese soy sauce
2 large eggs or 3 medium eggs
1⅓ cups (350 ml) Basic Dashi Stock (page 23) or ⅔ teaspoon *dashi* stock granules dissolved in 1⅓ cups (350 ml) hot water
1 teaspoon *mirin*
8 gingko nuts, peeled, blanched and skins removed (optional)
4 fresh shiitake mushrooms, stems discarded, caps left whole
4 fresh medium shrimp, peeled and deveined, heads and tails intact,
4 *mitsuba* or watercress stems, cut into sections
Grated *yuzu* orange or lemon peel, to garnish

1 Marinate the sliced chicken in 2 teaspoons of soy sauce for about 10 minutes. Drain and set aside.
2 To prepare the custard, break the eggs in a large bowl and stir gently with chopsticks or a fork. Do not beat or allow bubbles to form in the eggs. Combine the *dashi* stock with the remaining soy sauce in a saucepan and place over medium heat. Heat until almost to a boil, then quickly remove from the heat. Add the *mirin* and stir.
3 Pour the *dashi* mixture, while still hot, in a slow, steady stream into the eggs, stirring gently to blend. Strain the egg and *dashi* mixture through a fine sieve.
4 Evenly divide and place the chicken, followed by gingko nuts, mushroom caps, shrimp and *mitsuba* or watercress into four small but deep heat-proof cups or bowls. Slowly pour an equal amount of egg and *dashi* mixture down the side of the cups. Seal each cup with foil, a heat-proof plate or a lid.
5 Heat water in a large steamer, and place the custard cups on the rack. Steam over medium-high heat for 1 minute, then reduce the heat to low and steam for another 15 minutes. Insert a knife or fork into the custard; it is cooked when the knife or fork comes out clean. Remove from the steamer and garnish with the grated *yuzu* orange or lemon peel. Serve immediately.

Serves 4   Preparation time: 20 mins   Cooking time: 10 mins

Grilled Red Snapper Amadai Ito-Uni Yaki

Sea urchin, *uni*, is a much favored delicacy. Used in sushi, it is also very tasty blended with egg yolk and used as a topping for grilled seafood.

1 lb (500 g) red snapper fillet
½–1 teaspoon salt
2 tablespoons sake
3 egg yolks
²/₃ oz (20 g) sea urchin paste or 1½ oz (40 g) fresh sea urchin roe
2 tablespoons butter (optional)
Very finely sliced carrot, to garnish (optional)

1 Slice the fillet into eight portions, rub with salt and refrigerate for 1–2 hours.
2 Combine the egg yolks and sea urchin paste. Stir lightly to mix well.
3 Set the broiler at moderate heat (350°F/175°C). Skewer each piece of fish onto three skewers so that it holds its shape during grilling. Sprinkle the fish with sake and grill very quickly for a minute on each side. Brush the fish with the egg-sea urchin glaze and continue to grill until the glaze sets. Turn the fish over and brush again. Repeat three to four times, until the glaze is an even, golden yellow—this will take a total of 10 minutes. Do not overcook the fish. When the fish is almost done, brush it with butter, if using, and grill quickly on both sides.
4 Place the fish on a serving platter and remove the skewers carefully, twisting them slightly. Garnish with the sliced carrot and serve.

Note: Sea urchin paste is sold bottled. They are available in the refrigerated section in Japanese stores.

Serves 4   Preparation time: 15 mins + 1 hour to marinate   Cooking time: 10 mins

Abalone Simmered in Sake and Ginger

8–12 small fresh or canned abalone (about 7–10 oz/200–300 g)
½ cup (125 ml) Basic Dashi Stock (page 23) or ¼ teaspoon *dashi* stock
  granules dissolved in ½ cup (125 ml) hot water
1½ tablespoons sake
½–1 teaspoon sugar
½ teaspoon Japanese soy sauce
1 teaspoon grated young ginger
1 tablespoon *tamari* or dark soy sauce

1 Rinse the abalone well and blanch in hot water. Make criss-cross incisions on the back of each abalone.
2 Combine the *dashi* stock, sake, sugar, soy sauce, ginger and *tamari* in a small saucepan and bring to a boil. Add the abalone and simmer on low heat for 10 minutes. Remove the abalone and serve immediately.

Serves 4   Preparation time: 5 mins   Cooking time: 10 mins

Salmon Tofu Fritters   Sake No Tsumire-Age

The combination of delicately seasoned salmon and crispy tofu balls makes this a delightfully light and palate-pleasing dish.

7 oz (200 g) salmon fillet, coarsely chopped

1 cake (8 oz/250 g) firm tofu

1–2 teaspoons of minced *mitsuba* stems or parsley

2 fresh shiitake mushrooms, stems discarded and caps thinly sliced

1½-in (3-cm) piece carrot, halved and sliced into thin strips

1 large cloud ear fungus (or a few small ones), soaked to expand and thinly sliced

1 egg, lightly beaten

2 teaspoons Japanese soy sauce

½ teaspoon salt

1 teaspoon sugar

3 teaspoons cornstarch

Handful of *mitsuba* leaves or parsley, with stems attached (optional)

Cornstarch, for dusting

Oil, for deep-frying

Accompaniments
Japanese soy sauce
Prepared Japanese mustard paste

1 Place the chopped salmon in a large mixing bowl. Soak the tofu in water for 1 to 2 minutes, drain in a cloth-lined sieve, then squeeze out excess moisture by wrapping the tofu in the cloth and twisting tightly.
2 Add the tofu and the minced *mitsuba* to the salmon followed by the rest of the ingredients except for the *mitsuba* leaves and oil. Mix gently to combine.
3 Heat the oil in a wok on medium-high heat. Shape a tablespoon of the salmon mixture into a small ball. Deep-fry, turning frequently, until the ball is light golden brown. Repeat with the rest of the mixture, then drain well on paper towels.
4 Spray the *mitsuba* or parsley leaves with a little water, then dust with a little cornstarch. Deep-fry in hot oil for a few seconds or until the coating sets.
5 Portion the salmon balls into individual serving baskets or platters. Garnish with the fried *mitsuba* leaves and serve with the soy sauce and mustard on the side.

Serves 4   Preparation time: 25 mins   Cooking time: 20 mins

Shiitake Mushrooms Stuffed with Shrimp   Urajiro Shiitake

10 oz (300 g) fresh medium shrimp, peeled and deveined

16 fresh shiitake mushrooms, stems discarded

Cornstarch, for dusting

Handful of *mitsuba* leaves or parsley, with stems attached (optional)

Oil, for deep-frying

2 tablespoons daikon, grated and mixed with ¼ teaspoon ground red pepper, to serve

Sweet Soy Sauce
½ cup (125 ml) Basic Dashi Stock (page 23) or ¼ teaspoon dashi stock granules dissolved in ½ cup (125 ml) hot water

1–1½ tablespoons sugar

1–2 tablespoons Japanese soy sauce

1 To prepare the Sweet Soy Sauce, heat the *dashi* stock, sugar and soy sauce in a small saucepan, stirring until the sugar dissolves. Spoon into four small saucers and set aside.
2 Using a cleaver or the back of a heavy knife, bruise the shrimp, then mince finely. Alternatively, place the shrimp in a processor and blend. Press a little of the minced shrimp into each mushroom cap and dust with the cornstarch.
3 Deep-fry the mushrooms, a few at a time, in hot oil for 2 minutes. Drain on paper towels and place onto four individual serving plates. Spray the *mitsuba* or parsley leaves with a little water, then dust with a little cornstarch. Deep-fry in hot oil for a few seconds or until the coating sets. Garnish each serving of mushroom with the *mistuba* leaves, accompanied with ½ tablespoon of the grated daikon and little saucers of Sweet Soy Sauce. Serve immediately.

Serves 4   Preparation time: 15 mins   Cooking time: 10 mins

Crunchy Almond Shrimp   Ebi Aamondo-Age

An excellent modern Japanese dish using almonds rather than the more traditional broken noodles for a crunchy exterior coating.

12 large fresh shrimp, about 8 oz
  (250 g)
2 tablespoons cornstarch, for dusting
½ cup (125 ml) Tempura Batter
  (page 25)
1 cup (200 g) slivered almonds
4 fresh shiitake mushrooms, stalks
  discarded and caps cross-cut
8 small Japanese green peppers, or
  1 green bell pepper, cut into strips
Oil, for deep-frying
4 tablespoons finely grated daikon,
  to serve
Seven-spice chili powder (*shichimi*),
  to taste (optional)

Tempura Dipping Sauce
1 cup (250 ml) Basic Dashi Stock
  (page 23) or ½ teaspoon *dashi*
  stock granules dissolved in 1 cup
  (250 ml) hot water
1½ tablespoons Japanese soy sauce
3 tablespoons *mirin*

1 Make the Tempura Dipping Sauce by bringing all the ingredients to a boil in a small saucepan. Remove from the heat and cover to keep warm.
2 Trim the whiskers and legs of the shrimp with scissors. Peel the shrimp, keep the tails intact and reserve the heads. Make a small slit along the back of each shrimp and devein. Make several small incisions crosswise on the underside of each shrimp to prevent it from curling when fried. Pat dry and dust with cornstarch and set aside.
3 Heat the oil in a wok or saucepan. Dip each shrimp into the Tempura Batter and then press into the almond slivers to coat well. Deep-fry the shrimp until light golden brown. Drain on paper towels and set aside. Repeat with the shrimp heads.
4 Dust the shiitake mushrooms and green peppers with cornstarch, dip into the Tempura Batter and deep-fry. Drain on paper towels.
5 Arrange the fried shrimp, mushrooms and green peppers on four platters. Serve immediately with the grated daikon and bowls of warm dipping sauce on the side. Sprinkle each portion with the seven-spice chili powder if desired.

Note: Crunchy Sweet Potato Shrimp, another tasty variation, uses 1½ cups of coarsely grated sweet potato, tossed in 2 tablespoons of cornstarch in place of the slivered almonds. Dust the shrimp with a little cornstarch, then dip in lightly beaten egg white rather than the Tempura Batter before pressing into the sweet potato.

Serves 4   Preparation time: 20 mins   Cooking time: 20 mins

Deep-fried Crispy Whitebait   Shirauo Kara-Age

1 lb (500 g) fresh whitebait
½ cup (60 g) cornstarch
Oil, for deep-frying
Salt, to taste (optional)
1 lemon, cut into wedges, to serve
Ponzu Dipping Sauce (page 24),
  to serve

1 Rinse, drain and pat the whitebait dry, then place it in a small bowl or plastic bag with the cornstarch. Coat the whitebait with the cornstarch by mixing it gently or shaking the bag. Place the coated whitebait in a colander or sieve and shake gently to remove excess cornstarch.
2 Deep-fry a handful of the whitebait at a time in very hot oil until golden brown. Drain on paper towels and sprinkle with salt, if using. Serve with lemon wedges and the Ponzu Dipping Sauce on the side.

Note: Frozen whitebait is available in Japanese, Korean or well-stocked Asian supermarkets.

Serves 4–6   Preparation time: 5 mins   Cooking time: 10 mins

Baked Tuna Seasoned with Miso, Ginger and Kelp
Konbu-Yaki

Strips of dried kelp (*konbu*) are fashioned into little "boats" which hold the seasoned tuna during baking, adding flavor as well as an unusual appearance to this tasty fish dish.

4 sheets dried kelp (*konbu*), each measuring 6 x 3 in (15 x 8 cm)
10 oz (300 g) fresh tuna fillet or canned tuna, drained and flaked
3 spring onions, finely sliced
1½ tablespoons grated young ginger
8 small Japanese green peppers, sliced, or 1 green bell pepper, diced

White Dengaku Miso Sauce
½ cup (100 g) white miso
1¾ tablespoons sake
1¾ tablespoons *mirin*
1½ tablespoons sugar
3 tablespoons water

1 To make the White Dengaku Miso Sauce, place all the ingredients in a saucepan, and simmer over medium heat, stirring constantly. When it comes to almost a boil, reduce the heat to very low and simmer for 10 minutes, stirring from time to time. Transfer to a bowl and set aside to cool.
2 Wipe the kelp with a damp cloth. Place it in a shallow tray and pour just enough water to immerse. Remove the kelp when it is soft and pliable. Cut several very narrow strips from the sides of each piece of the kelp to use as strings for tying. Accordion-fold both ends and tie each end with the kelp string so that it resembles a boat.
3 Combine the tuna, spring onions, ginger, Miso Sauce and half the chopped peppers, mixing well. Portion the tuna mixture into each kelp boat and top with the remaining green peppers. Preheat the oven to 350°F (175°C), then bake the kelp boats for 15 minutes. Serve hot with rice.

Note: Alternatively, bake the fish in an small, shallow baking dish lined with the sheets of kelp after they have been wiped clean with a damp cloth and soaked briefly to expand.

Serves 4   Preparation time: 30 mins   Cooking time: 15 mins

Grilled Miso Cod   Managatsuo Saikyo-Yaki

This is an exquisite way to prepare white fish fillets like cod, seabass or snapper. For maximum flavor, begin preparing this dish 3 days in advance, as the fish fillets are much better if marinated for this length of time before being grilled.

1–1½ lbs (500–750 g) cod or sea-bass fillets
1½ cups (300 g) white miso
⅓ cup (85 ml) sake
½ tablespoon sugar
½ teaspoon ground red pepper (optional)
2 tablespoons *mirin*, for basting
4 oz (125 g) daikon radish (about 2 in/5 cm), freshly grated or 4 pieces pickled daikon, to serve
Japanese soy sauce, to serve

1 Cut the fish into four serving pieces. Combine the miso, sake, sugar and ground red pepper (if using) in a bowl. Add the fish fillets and rub the marinade into the fish so that they are well coated. Cover and marinate in the refrigerator for 1–3 days.
2 Remove the fillets and scrape off the miso. Cut a shallow cross on the surface of each fillet and broil under low heat for about 20 minutes or until the fish is cooked. Brush the fillets with *mirin* each time you turn them over to add a shiny glaze to the fish. Serve immediately with the grated or pickled daikon and soy sauce on the side.

Serves 4   Preparation time: 5 mins + 1 day to marinate   Cooking time: 20 mins

Grilled Clams with Miso and Mushrooms

Hamaguri No Kogane-Yaki

16 large clams
8 fresh shiitake mushrooms, stems
  discarded, caps quartered
2 tablespoons Japanese Mayonnaise
  (page 25)
½ tablespoon white miso
½ teaspoon finely grated *yuzu*
  orange or lemon peel

1 Steam the clams using lightly salted water and remove from the heat immediately when the shells open. Drain the clams and remove the meat, reserving the shells. Cut each clam in half. Put 2 clam pieces and mushrooms on each reserved shell.
2 Mix the Japanese Mayonnaise, miso and *yuzu* peel together and top each clam shell with about ½ teaspoon of the mixture. Grill under low heat for 2 minutes, then serve immediately.

Note: If using bottled Japanese mayonnaise, add 1 tablespoon white miso, ½ teaspoon lemon juice or a pinch of grated citrus peel.

Serves 4   Preparation time: 8 mins   Cooking time: 2 mins

Barbequed Eel   Unagi Kaba-Yaki

This is one of the most popular dishes in Japan, particularly in the summer. These days, prepared eel and its grilling sauce are easily available in Japanese and Korean supermarkets.

10 oz (300 g) cooked and prepared
  eel or 1 lb (500 g) fresh eel fillets
Ready-made young pickled bamboo
  shoots, to serve
Sansho powder, to serve

Seafood Glazing Sauce
3 tablespoons sake
2 tablespoons *mirin*
2 tablespoons Japanese soy sauce
4 teaspoons sugar
½ cup (125 ml) fish stock

1 To prepare the Seafood Glazing Sauce, place all the ingredients in a pan and bring to a boil. Reduce the heat to low, skim the surface and continue simmering until the sauce has reduced by half. Set aside.
2 Thread two or three long skewers through the prepared or fresh eel so that it keeps its shape while cooking. Place the skewered eel on a hot charcoal grill under a broiler, meat side facing the heat. Grill for 3 minutes and turn so that the skin faces the heat. Grill for another 3 minutes.
3 Brush the eel with the prepared Glazing Sauce and grill each side for a little over 1 minute. Repeat several times, about 1 minute on each side, basting with the glaze each time. Place the cooked eel on a cutting board. Twist the skewers and pull them out gently. Slice the eel into 4-in (10-cm) pieces and arrange on a platter, served hot with the pickled bamboo shoots and sprinkle with the *sansho* powder.

Note: To make fish stock, grill eel bones or the bones of any fish (3 oz/90 g) until they turn whitish, then put them in a pan with 1 cup (250 ml) water and boil for 5 minutes. Strain, discarding the solids and reserve.

Serves 4   Preparation time: 10 mins   Cooking time: 25 mins

Grilled Whole Fish with Salt Karei Shio-Yaki

This is perhaps the simplest and also the tastiest method of cooking whole fish. Pressing the fish liberally with salt before grilling helps keep in the moisture and gives the fish an attractive snowy coat. Grilled fish is usually served with grated daikon on the side, drizzled with soy sauce, and eaten with hot steamed rice.

4 small to medium whole fish, such
  as mackerel, trout, flounder, sole or
  pomfret
1 tablespoon coarse salt
Lemon wedge, to garnish
4 oz (125 g) daikon radish (about
  2 in/5 cm), grated and lightly
  squeezed to remove moisture

Pickled Lotus Root
½ cup peeled and thinly sliced lotus
  root
3 tablespoons Sweet Vinegar
  (page 24)
1 red chili, deseeded
¼ cup (75 ml) Ponzu Dipping Sauce
  (page 24)

1 Prepare the Pickled Lotus Root in advance as it needs to marinate. Blanch the sliced lotus root in water for 30 seconds, drain and place it in the Sweet Vinegar. Heat the chili in a dry pan for a few seconds, then add it to the Sweet Vinegar. Pour in the Ponzu Dipping Sauce. Stir and refrigerate for several hours.
2 Clean, scale and rinse the fish thoroughly. Dry with a paper towel and make two deep incisions crosswise on each side. Put a skewer through the fish. Sprinkle both sides of the fish lightly with salt, then press a liberal amount of salt onto the tail and fins.
3 Cook the fish over a moderately hot charcoal fire or under a broiler, turning it with the skewer to avoid damaging the skin, until the fish is golden on both sides and cooked through. Turn the fish only once. Wrap the tail in aluminum foil halfway through to avoid it getting too charred, if necessary. Serve on a plate garnished with the lemon wedge, grated daikon and Japanese soy sauce with the Pickled Lotus Root on the side.

Note: If using a long, narrow fish, put the skewer through the tail end of and out through the center, then through the head so that the fish has an "S" wave shape.

Serves 2–4   Preparation time: 20 mins   Cooking time: 15 mins

Baked Scallops with Miso in an Orange Cup
Hotate Yuzu Kama-Yaki

10 oz (300 g) fresh scallops, quartered, or shrimp, peeled and deveined
4 *yuzu* oranges or small mandarin
  oranges
Baby daikon radish, blanched in
  lightly salted water, to serve
4 teaspoons red miso, to serve

Red Dengaku Miso Sauce
3 tablespoons red miso
1½ tablespoons sake
1½ tablespoons *mirin*
½–1 tablespoon sugar
3 tablespoons water

1 To make the Red Dengaku Miso Sauce, combine all the ingredients in a small saucepan and gently heat on low for 5 to 10 minutes, stirring constantly until the sugar has dissolved. Turn off the heat and set the saucepan aside.
2 In a mixing bowl, combine the scallop pieces with the Red Dengaku Miso Sauce. Cut off the top of each *yuzu* or orange and reserve as a lid. Hollow out the rest of the *yuzu* or orange carefully. Portion and fill each orange cup with the scallop mixture.
3 Preheat the oven to 350°F (175°C). Set the lid aside and bake the filled orange cups for 15 minutes. Serve warm, covered with the reserved lids, and accompanied with the cooked *daikon* and the miso.

Serves 4   Preparation time: 40 mins   Cooking time: 15 mins

Baked Scallops and Mushrooms in an Apple

Hotate Ringo Kama-Yaki

4 small red apples

10 oz (300 g) scallops, rinsed and patted dry

4 fresh shiitake mushrooms

4 small Japanese green peppers or ½ green bell pepper

1 teaspoon oil

Pinch of freshly ground black pepper, to taste

2 tablespoons Japanese Mayonnaise (page 25)

1½–2 tablespoons white miso

½ teaspoon grated *yuzu* or lemon rind

1 Cut ½ in (1 cm) from the top of each apple and reserve as lids. Using a paring knife, carefully remove and discard the core. Then, use a melon baller to hollow out each apple, leaving about ½ in (1 cm) of flesh on the sides and about 1½ in (3 cm) at the bottom. Submerge the apples in ice water with a little salt to prevent them from discoloring.

2 Cut the scallops, mushrooms and peppers into small cubes. Heat the oil in a skillet and stir-fry until the scallops turn white. Season with pepper and place into a mixing bowl. Combine the mayonnaise and miso with the grated rind, then stir with the stir-fried scallops and vegetables to mix well.

3 Preheat the oven to 350°F (175°C). Stuff each apple with equal portions of this filling. Bake the apples in the oven for 25 minutes. Serve hot with the lids on the side.

Serves 4   Preparation time: 20 mins   Cooking time: 20 mins

Grilled Fish Rolls Stuffed with Burdock

7 oz (200 g) burdock root

1 cup (250 ml) Cold Soba Dashi Broth (page 23)

½ cup (125 ml) water

4 teaspoons sugar

1 lb (500 g) mackerel or Atlantic hairtail fillets

3 tablespoons Seafood Glazing Sauce (page 83)

Baby daikon radish, peeled and boiled in lightly salted water for 5 minutes, to serve

Sansho powder, to taste

1 Clean the burdock, slice into quarters lengthwise and cut each quarter into 5-in (12-cm) sticks. Bring the Cold Soba Dashi Broth, water and sugar to a boil in a saucepan. Add the burdock and boil for about 20 minutes, or until the burdock is soft enough to be pierced by a fork. Drain and cool.

2 Cut the fish fillets into long strips that are about ½ in (1 cm) thick. Take three sticks of boiled burdock and wind a strip of fish around them to form a tight bundle. Fasten the bundles by inserting two or three skewers across the burdock sticks. Continue until all the burdock sticks and fish fillets are used up.

3 Grill the wrapped burdock bundles under a broiler or over a charcoal fire for about 10 minutes or until the fish is cooked, brushing the outside with Seafood Glazing Sauce and turning over three or four times to brown evenly.

4 Remove the skewers and cut the rolls into ¾-in (2-cm) pieces. Serve with the cooked daikon and a sprinkling of the *sansho* pepper.

Serves 4   Preparation time: 40 mins   Cooking time: 20 mins

Chicken Rolls with Sour Plum   Toriniku No Bainiku Age

The salty, sour plums (*umeboshi*) so popular in Japan make a surprise filling in these chicken rolls, which are decoratively wrapped either with a *shiso* leaf or a piece of *nori* seaweed. Like the plums, the *shiso* and *nori* also add a tasty and rather unusual accent to regular fried chicken.

14 oz (400 g) chicken breast, skin removed
2 sour plums (*umeboshi*)
½ teaspoon salt
8 *shiso* leaves
2 teaspoons cornstarch blended with a little hot water to make a paste
1 sheet of toasted *nori*, about 8 x 7 in (20 x 18 cm)
Oil, for deep-frying
Cornstarch, for dusting
Wedges of lime or lemon, to garnish

1 Cut the chicken breast into 16 finger-sized strips. Make a small slit in the middle of each strip, taking care not to cut all the way through the flesh.
2 Remove the stone from each plum and use a spoon to break it into eight small pieces. Stuff a piece of plum into the pocket cut in each chicken strip. Sprinkle the chicken with salt.
3 Wrap a *shiso* leaf around a piece of the chicken, sealing the ends with a little of the blended cornstarch. Repeat until the *shiso* leaves are used up.
4 Cut the *nori* sheet into eight long strips. Roll a *nori* strip around a piece of the remaining chicken, sealing the ends with a little constarch paste. Repeat until the *nori* strips are used up.
5 Heat the oil in a wok. In the meantime, lightly dust the chicken rolls with the cornstarch, shake off excess cornstarch and set aside. When the oil is very hot, reduce the heat to medium, and deep-fry, a few at a time, for 4 to 5 minutes or until light golden brown. Serve hot, garnished with wedges of lime or lemon.

Serves 4   Preparation time: 15 mins   Cooking time: 20 mins

Chicken Wings and Potatoes Braised in Ginger and Soy
Tebasaki To Sato-Imo

This dish is made using *sato-imo*, also known as taro potatoes, which have a delicious creamy texture when thoroughly cooked. As *sato-imo* are not readily available, baby potatoes—or any boiling potato or yams—may be used instead. Tasty and easy to prepare, more vegetables can be added to make a complete one-dish meal.

1 lb (500 g) chicken wings
3 tablespoons sake
2 teaspoons oil
¾ in (2 cm) young ginger, sliced
5 spring onions, cut into sections
14 oz (400 g) baby potatoes or *sato-imo* potatoes, peeled
2–3 tablespoons Japanese soy sauce
2 teaspoons dark soy sauce or *tamari* soy sauce
2–3 teaspoons sugar
12 snow peas or sugar snap peas

1 Marinate the chicken wings in the sake for 30 minutes. Heat the oil in a pan and stir-fry the wings until they change color. Add the ginger, spring onions and enough water to just cover the chicken. Cover the pan and simmer for 5 minutes.
2 Add the potatoes, soy sauce and sugar, and stir. Simmer, covered, over medium heat for 20 minutes or until the potatoes are soft.
3 Blanch the snow peas in lightly salted water and set aside.
4 Dish the chicken wings and potatoes into four bowls and serve warm with snow peas on the side.

Serves 4   Preparation time: 15 mins   Cooking time: 20 mins

Fried Pork Cutlets on Rice Katsudon

These delicious fried cutlets (*tonkatsu*) make a wonderfully satisfying lunch served with a bowl of rice, a dollop of hot prepared mustard, some thinly sliced cabbage and a splash of *tonkatsu* sauce. *Tonkatsu* sauce is a thick, dark brown sauce with a fruity and slightly sour flavor reminiscent of Worcestershire or steak sauce. The fried cutlets can also be topped with sweet, crunchy onions and a *dashi*-based egg gravy.

4 cups (600 g) cooked rice
4 sprigs *mitsuba* or parsley, to
   garnish (optional)
Prepared Japanese mustard, to serve
Tonkatsu sauce, to serve (optional)

Pork Cutlets
1 lb (500 g) pork loin or pork steaks,
   preferably with the fat left on
Salt and pepper, to taste
2 tablespoons cornstarch
1 egg, lightly beaten
½ cup bread crumbs
Oil, for deep-frying

Sauce
2 teaspoons oil
3 medium onions, thinly sliced
1 cup (250 ml) Basic Dashi Stock
   (page 23) or ½ teaspoon *dashi*
   stock granules dissolved in 1 cup
   (250 ml) hot water
4 tablespoons *mirin*
4 tablespoons Japanese soy sauce
4 teaspoons sugar
2 eggs, lightly beaten (optional)

1 Prepare the Pork Cutlets first by cutting the pork loin into four steaks. Make small incisions along the fatty edges to prevent the steaks from curling during frying. Season the meat lightly with salt and pepper, dust with cornstarch on both sides, dip in the beaten egg and then press into the bread crumbs. Heat the oil in a wok or a saucepan until moderately hot. Deep-fry the crumb-coated cutlets until light golden brown and cooked, for about 3–4 minutes on each side. Drain on paper towels and set aside.
2 To prepare the Sauce, heat the oil in a skillet and fry the onions for 2 minutes. Remove the onions and set aside. Add the *dashi* stock, *mirin*, soy sauce and sugar in a pan. Stir and simmer on high heat for 5 minutes. Add the onions, stir and remove the skillet from the heat. Add the beaten eggs, if using and stir gently. Set aside.
3 Scoop the rice into four large bowls and pour the Sauce and onions over it. Place a cutlet into each bowl, garnish with the *mitsuba* or parsley. Serve hot, accompanied with pickles of your choice (see page 26), mustard and *tonkatsu* sauce, if desired.

Note: Bottled *tonkatsu* sauce is widely available in Asian food stores and well-stocked supermarkets. Alternatively, make your own using 1 part Worcestershire or steak sauce and 5 parts tomato ketchup.

Serves 4   Preparation time: 20 mins   Cooking time: 15 mins

Pork Stir-fried with Ginger and Vegetables
Butaniku Shoga-Yaki

1 lb (500 g) pork loin
1 tablespoon oil
1 large onion, halved lengthwise and
   cut into thin slices
7 oz (200 g) cabbage cut into
   squares
1 cup (200 g) Japanese green
   peppers or bell peppers, deseeded
   and cut into squares

Seasoning
4 teaspoons juice of grated young
   ginger
2–3 tablespoons Japanese soy sauce
1 teaspoon dark soy sauce or *tamari*
   soy sauce
2–3 teaspoons sugar
3 tablespoons sake

1 Prepare the Seasoning by mixing the ginger juice, soy sauces, sugar and sake together in a small bowl. Set aside.
2 Slice the pork into very thin pieces. To thinly slice the pork, wrap it in plastic and place it in the freezer for 20 minutes or until it is half-frozen. Remove the plastic and slice the pork across the grain with a very sharp knife into very thin sheets.
3 Heat ½ tablespoon oil in a frying pan or wok. Stir-fry the onions over high heat for 1 minute, then add the cabbage and green peppers and stir-fry for another 2 minutes. Remove and set aside.
4 In the same pan, heat the remaining oil. Add the pork and stir-fry over very high heat for 5 minutes, or until it is cooked. Add the Seasoning and stir, then add the vegetables, mix well and serve hot with steamed rice and soup, if desired.

Serves 4–6   Preparation time: 20 mins   Cooking time: 10 mins

Seasoned Chicken Loaf   Tori No Matsukaze

Tiny poppy seeds scattered over the top of this seasoned chicken loaf are supposedly reminiscent of sand on a beach. In this dish, also known as "Wind in the Pines," sesame seeds can be used in place of poppy seeds if these are not available.

14 oz (400 g) boneless chicken
2 eggs, lightly beaten
2 teaspoons minced young ginger
2 tablespoons red miso
2 teaspoons sake
2 teaspoons Japanese soy sauce
2 tablespoons sugar
2 teaspoons cornstarch
1 tablespoon fine white poppy seeds
   or sesame seeds
8-in (20-cm) square baking pan
Bamboo sticks or ice-cream sticks
   (optional)

1 Grind the chicken in a food processor to make a paste. Add all the other ingredients except the poppy or sesame seeds and process until well mixed.
2 Line the base and the sides of an 8-in (20-cm) square baking pan with baking paper or oiled foil. Put in the chicken mixture, spreading evenly, then sprinkle with the poppy seeds. Preheat the oven to 350°F (175°C). Set the baking pan with the chicken into a larger heat-proof tray half-filled with water and bake for about 30 minutes, until the center is firm.
3 Remove the pan from the oven and pull up the sides of the baking paper or foil to lift the loaf out of the pan. Cut the loaf into rectangles or fan shapes and skewer onto the sticks. Serve at room temperature.

Serves 4–6   Preparation time: 15 mins   Cooking time: 30 mins

Chicken with Asparagus   Tori To Asupara Karashi-Ae

This easily prepared dish combines lightly poached chicken with asparagus and creamy seasoned Japanese Mayonnaise.

12 oz (350 g) skinless chicken breast
8 fresh asparagus spears, cut into
   sections
Toasted white sesame seeds, to
   garnish (optional)

Creamy Japanese Mayonnaise
   Dressing
4 tablespoons Japanese Mayonnaise
   (page 25)
1–2 teaspoons prepared Japanese
   hot mustard paste
¼ teaspoon salt
¼ teaspoon white pepper

1 Poach the chicken for 5–7 minutes in boiling water until the meat is just cooked. Drain and plunge in ice water for a few seconds. Cut or tear the cooled chicken into lengths and set aside.
2 Blanch the asparagus in lightly salted water for 1 or 2 minutes until just tender. Drain and plunge in ice water for a few seconds. Drain and set aside.
3 Make the Creamy Japanese Mayonnaise Dressing by combining all the ingredients in a small bowl. Mix well and set aside.
4 This dish can be eaten chilled or at room temperature. Just before serving, portion the chicken and asparagus pieces into four individual bowls and top with the prepared dressing. Garnish with a sprinkling of sesame seeds.

Note: If using bottled Japanese mayonnaise, add 1 tablespoon white miso and ½ teaspoon lemon juice and the rest of the ingredients listed for the Dressing and mix well.

Serves 4   Preparation time: 15 mins   Cooking time: 10 mins

Simmered Duck or Pork with Vegetables   Kamo Jibu-Ni

12 oz (350 g) duck breast (with skin)
   or pork loin
4 dried shiitake mushrooms, soaked
   in hot water for 10 minutes to soften,
   stems discarded
1½ cups (375 ml) Basic Dashi Stock
   (page 23) or ¾ teaspoon *dashi*
   stock granules dissolved in 1½ cups
   (375 ml) hot water
¼ cup (60 ml) *mirin*
¼ cup (60 ml) Japanese soy sauce
1½ tablespoons sugar
Wasabi paste, to serve

Simmered Greens
10 oz (300 g) rape or broccoli blossoms or snow peas, washed and
   trimmed, stems removed
½ cup (125 ml) Basic Dashi Stock
   or ¼ teaspoon *dashi* stock granules
   dissolved in ½ cup (125 ml) hot
   water
1 teaspoon *mirin*
1 teaspoon Japanese soy sauce
Salt, to taste

Simmered Potatoes
1 lb (500 g) baby potatoes or *sato-
   imo* potatoes
1 cup (250 ml) Basic Dashi Stock
   (page 23) or ¼ teaspoon *dashi*
   stock granules dissolved in 1 cup
   (250 ml) hot water
1½ teaspoons Japanese soy sauce
½ teaspoon sugar
½ teaspoon salt
Yuzu orange or lemon peel, to garnish
   (optional)

1 Cut the duck or pork into thick slices. If using duck, cut a few incisions into the duck skin.
2 Bring the *dashi* stock, *mirin,* soy sauce and sugar to a boil in a saucepan, add the meat and shiitake mushrooms and simmer over low heat for 10–15 minutes until the meat is cooked. Turn off the heat, remove the meat slices and mushrooms with a slotted spoon and set aside. Continue to simmer the stock for another 5 minutes or more until the stock is reduced to a syrupy sauce. Keep warm and set aside.
3 To make the Simmered Greens, blanch the rape or broccoli blossoms or snow peas in lightly salted boiling water. Drain, cool under a running tap and drain again. Set aside. Pour the *dashi* stock, *mirin*, soy sauce and salt in a saucepan and bring to a boil. Turn off the heat. Add the vegetables to the stock and let it stand for 30 seconds to 1 minute, remove from the heat and drain.
4 To make the Simmered Potatoes, peel the potatoes and cut them into irregular chunks. If using baby potatoes, pan-fry in a little oil until they are lightly browned. Remove from the heat, drain on paper towels and set aside. If using *sato-imo* potatoes, simmer in water for 10 minutes until just tender and drain. Place the potatoes in a saucepan together with the *dashi* stock, soy sauce, sugar and salt. Bring to a boil and simmer over low heat for 5 to 10 minutes, or until the potatoes are cooked. Dish into serving bowls, garnish with bits of grated orange or lemon, and set aside.
5 Arrange the meat, mushrooms and the Simmered Greens in individual serving bowls and top with warm sauce (set aside in step 2). Serve immediately with a dollop of wasabi, together with the potatoes.

Serves 4   Preparation time: 30 mins   Cooking time: 45 mins

Sirloin Steak Teriyaki Teriyaki Suteki

8 small Japanese green peppers,
  or 1 large green bell pepper, cut
  into 8 strips
1 lb (500 g) beef tenderloin, cut into
  bite-sized cubes

Fried Vegetables
1 teaspoon oil
2 cups (150 g) bean sprouts
1 cup fresh oyster mushrooms, ends
  trimmed or fresh shiitake mushrooms, stems discarded
1 tablespoon sake
¼ teaspoon freshly ground black
  pepper
½ teaspoon salt

Teriyaki Steak Sauce
6½ tablespoons Japanese soy sauce
6½ tablespoons sake
⅔ cup (150 ml) *mirin*
2 tablespoons sugar

1 Prepare the Teriyaki Steak Sauce first by combining all the ingredients in a saucepan and bringing to a boil over medium heat. Simmer for about 10–15 minutes until the sauce is reduced to about 1 cup (250 ml).
2 If using Japanese green peppers, make a small slit in the side of each. Thread the Japanese peppers or bell pepper strips onto skewers and grill until done.
3 Thread the steak on skewers and grill until about half-cooked. Brush with the Teriyaki Steak Sauce and return to the grill for another 30 seconds or so. Turn the steak over and brush again. Grill for another 30 seconds, then give the steak a final brushing and cook for 30 seconds on each side until nicely glazed.
4 To cook the Fried Vegetables, heat the pan over high heat, add the oil and stir-fry the bean sprouts and mushrooms briskly. Season with the sake, pepper and salt. Stir-fry for 1–2 minutes, or until just cooked. Portion into individual serving plates.
5 Remove the skewers from the peppers and steak and serve immediately with the vegetables on the side.

Serves 4   Preparation time: 15 mins   Cooking time: 10 mins

Stuffed Lotus Root or Eggplant Tempura

This dish is like a sandwich with a filling of seasoned ground pork—which can be prepared in advance—between slices of lotus root or eggplant. The "sandwich" is then dipped in a tempura batter and deep-fried.

8 oz (250 g) lotus root, peeled, sliced
  and kept in water or 10 oz (300 g)
  slender Japanese eggplant, sliced
  diagonally
Cornstarch, for dusting
Tempura Batter (page 25)
Oil, for deep-frying
Salt and pepper, to taste
Prepared Japanese mustard paste
  (optional), to serve

Pork Filling
7 oz (200 g) ground pork
4 tablespoons minced onion
2 teaspoons cornstarch
1 egg, lightly beaten
1 teaspoon Japanese soy sauce

Tempura Dipping Sauce
1 cup (250 ml) Basic Dashi Stock
  (page 23) or ½ teaspoon *dashi*
  stock granules dissolved in 1 cup
  (250 ml) hot water
1½ tablespoons Japanese soy sauce
3 tablespoons *mirin*

1 Make the Tempura Dipping Sauce by bringing all the ingredients to a boil in a small saucepan. Remove from the heat and cover to keep warm.
2 Prepare the Pork Filling by combining all the ingredients and mixing well.
3 Pat the lotus root slices dry and dust both sides with a little cornstarch. Place some of the Pork Filling on a lotus root slice and top with another slice of root, and press lightly and set aside on a dry plate. Repeat until all the lotus root is used up.
4 Prepare the Tempura Batter. Heat the oil in a wok until moderately hot. Dip the pork-filled vegetable slices in the batter and deep-fry until golden brown on both sides. Drain on paper towels and sprinkle with a little salt and pepper.
5 Serve immediately accompanied with warm Tempura Dipping Sauce and Japanese mustard, if desired.

Serves 4–6   Preparation time: 20 mins   Cooking time: 15 mins

Seared Tataki Beef   Gyuniku No Tataki

1 lb (500 g) beef sirloin, cut into 4
  sections
1 teaspoon salt
1 medium onion
Ohba or *shiso* leaves or sprigs of
  watercress, to garnish
7 oz (200 g) daikon radish (about 3 in/
  8 cm), peeled and very thinly sliced
Thinly sliced spring onions, to garnish
4 tablespoons finely grated daikon
  mixed with ¼ teaspoon ground red
  pepper, to serve
Ponzu Dipping Sauce (page 24),
  to serve

1 Heat a skillet until very hot. Sprinkle the beef with salt and sear it for a few
seconds on each side, just until the color changes. Remove and cut into
very thin slices.
2 Peel the onion, cut in half lengthwise, then into very thin slices across.
Break up the slices with your fingers and put in ice water to chill. Rinse,
drain and dry the onion slices.
3 To serve, lay the beef slices in a circle on a large platter. Arrange the
greens in the center, topped with the sliced daikon and onions. Garnish with
spring onions and place small mounds of the grated daikon on the side.
Serve with a small bowl of the Ponzu Dipping Sauce.

Serves 4   Preparation time: 10 mins   Cooking time: 5 mins

Cold Dashi Custard Tofu   Tamago Dofu

This chilled custard makes a refreshing summer appetizer, and looks as lovely as it tastes when garnished with
sprigs of *shiso* flowers or leaves. If these are not available, use decorative sprigs or petals of any edible flowers.
Flowering basil is one such good substitute.

3 eggs, lightly beaten
¾ cup (175 ml) Basic Dashi Stock
  (page 23) or ½ teaspoon *dashi*
  stock granules dissolved in ¾ cup
  hot water
1–1½ tablespoons Japanese soy
  sauce
1 teaspoon *mirin*
4 medium cooked shrimp (optional)
⅔ cup (150 ml) Cold Soba Dashi
  Broth (page 23)
Grated *yuzu* orange, lime or lemon
  peel, to garnish
Shiso flowers or thinly sliced *shiso*
  leaves, to garnish

1 Combine the eggs, *dashi* stock, soy sauce and *mirin* in a bowl and stir the
mixture gently. Pour it into a small, square or rectangular, heat-proof bowl or
dish measuring about 4 in (10 cm) on each side. Steam over medium heat for
about 25 minutes until it sets. Set aside to cool, cover and chill until needed.
2 Slice the custard into four, and place each piece in a small glass or china
bowl. Place a shrimp, if using, on top of each piece of custard and spoon
the Cold Soba Dashi Broth over it. Garnish with the grated citrus peel and
shiso flowers or leaves. Serve chilled.

Serves 4   Preparation time: 10 mins   Cooking time: 25 mins

Sukiyaki   Beef Hotpot with Vegetables

One of the most popular Japanese dishes abroad, sukiyaki became known in Japan around the turn of the century, when the Japanese began eating beef (previously prohibited by Buddhist law). There are two styles of sukiyaki: the Osaka style involves preparing the Sukiyaki Sauce at the table each time a new ingredient is cooked; in the Tokyo style (followed in this recipe) the sauce is made in advance, and served with the cooked food.

1 lb (500 g) well-marbled prime beef sirloin, very thinly sliced

1 packet (3 oz/90 g) dried *shirataki* or bean thread noodles or arrowroot starch noodles

1 large onion, peeled and thinly sliced

2 leeks, white part only, sliced diagonally

1 bunch chrysanthemum leaves, hard parts of stems discarded, washed

12 fresh shiitake mushrooms, stems discarded, caps cross-cut

4 oz (125 g) *enokitake* mushrooms, hard part of stems discarded

1 cake (8 oz/250 g) firm tofu, sliced into rectangles

1 gluten cake (*fu*) or grilled bean curd (*yakidofu*), sliced into rectangles

4 eggs (optional), to serve

1 portion Sukiyaki Sauce (page 24)

1 Prepare the Sukiyaki Sauce by following the instructions on page 24.

2 To thinly slice the beef, wrap it in shrinkwrap and place it in the freezer for 20 minutes or until it is half-frozen. Remove the plastic, slice and reserve some beef fat to use for greasing the pot later. Slice the beef across the grain with a very sharp knife into very thin sheets.

3 Cook the noodles in boiling water until soft (see packet instructions). Drain, rinse in cold water, drain again and set aside.

4 Arrange the beef, cooked noodles, vegetables and tofu on a large platter or basket. Crack the eggs into individual dipping bowls.

5 Place a large iron skillet or Dutch oven on top of a hot plate or gas burner on the table. Heat the pot and grease with a chunk of the reserved beef fat or small amount of vegetable oil. Add a small portion of the sliced beef and vegetables and tofu, pour a little of the Sukiyaki Sauce over the ingredients and simmer. When the ingredients are cooked, each person helps himself to the food from the hotpot. If desired, the food can be dipped into the lightly stirred egg before eating. Serve with steamed rice.

Serves 4   Preparation time: 30 mins   Cooking time: 30 mins

Oyster and Miso Hotpot   Dotenabe

In this dish, the casserole is lined with a layer of miso all around the edges of the pot, a method which has given this hotpot its name—*dotenabe* means "riverbank" in Japanese. *Dotenabe* is a typical dish from Hiroshima.

4 oz (125 g) daikon radish (2 in/5 cm),
   peeled, sliced in 1 in (½ cm) rounds
½ small carrot, top portion only,
   peeled, sliced into rounds
½ small Chinese cabbage
2 leeks, white part only, sliced
1 bunch chrysanthemum leaves, hard
   parts of stems discarded, washed
8 fresh shiitake mushrooms, stems
   discarded, caps cross-cut
3½ oz (100 g) *enokitake* mushrooms
1 cake (1 lb/500 g) silken tofu, cubed
24 freshly shucked oysters
2–3 tablespoons *inaka* miso or miso
⅓ cup (70 g) white miso
4 cups (1 liter) Basic Dashi Stock
   (page 23) or 2 teaspoons dashi
   stock granules dissolved in 4 cups
   (1 liter) hot water
Ponzu Dipping Sauce (page 24), to
   serve

1 Blanch the sliced daikon and carrots in lightly salted water. Slice the cabbage into large sections and the leeks on the diagonal. Arrange the prepared vegetables, mushrooms, tofu and oysters on a large platter.

2 Mix the two types of miso together and spread a layer of the miso mixture (about ¼ in/½ cm thick) around the side of a wide, heat-proof casserole dish.

3 Bring the *dashi* stock almost to a boil in a saucepan. Gently pour the stock into the middle of the casserole. Place the casserole on a heated hot plate or gas burner, set on medium, in the center of a table. Add the ingredients piece by piece to the boiling soup. Each person mixes a little miso into the soup from the edges of the casserole by brushing it with a morsel of food before eating. Serve with Ponzu Dipping Sauce on the side.

Serves 4   Preparation time: 40 mins   Cooking time: 30 mins

Shabu-Shabu   Mongolian Hotpot

1 lb (500 g) well-marbled, prime beef
  sirloin
1 packet (3½ oz/100 g) dried *shirataki*
  or bean thread noodles (optional)
10 oz (300 g) Chinese cabbage
2 leeks, white part only
1 bunch (8 oz/250 g) chrysanthemum
  leaves, washed, hard stems discarded
7 oz (200 g) *enokitake* mushrooms
8 fresh shiitake mushrooms, stems
  discarded, caps cross-cut
1 cake (8 oz/250 g) silken tofu, cubed

Stock
6 cups (1½ liters) water
1 strip dried kelp (*konbu*), (4 in/10 cm
  long), wiped with a damp cloth and
  halved
1 teaspoon salt

Accompaniments
Ponzu Dipping Sauce (page 24)
4 tablespoons finely grated daikon
  with ¼ teaspoon ground red pepper
Sesame Dipping Sauce (page 24)
4 tablespoons minced spring onions

1 Prepare both dipping sauces by following the instructions on page 24
and place into separate dipping bowls. Place the grated daikon and spring
onions into individual saucers.

2 Slice the beef following the instructions on page 100. Cook the noodles, if
using, in boiling water until soft (see packet instructions). Drain, rinse in cold
water, drain again and set aside.

3 Slice the cabbage thinly, keeping the leaves and stems separate. Slice
the leeks on the diagonal. Slice the hard ends of the *enokitake* mushroom
stems and discard. Arrange the beef, noodles, vegetables and tofu on a
serving platter or basket.

4 To prepare the Stock, place a large metal or ceramic casserole on a hot
plate or gas burner in the center of the table and add the water and kelp.
When the water comes to a boil, quickly remove the kelp with chopsticks
and discard. Add the salt and stir to dissolve.

5 Each person may now select morsels of food and immerse it in the Stock
with chopsticks until it is cooked. Skim the Stock of any foam that surfaces
during cooking. Have some boiling water at hand, to add to the Stock while
cooking, should it dry up too quickly. The noodles are usually cooked last, by
which time the Stock would have become a rich soup. Serve with the Ponzu
Dipping Sauce mixed with the grated daikon, and the Sesame Dipping
Sauce mixed with the spring onions.

Serves 4–6   Preparation time: 30 mins   Cooking time: 30 mins

Mixed Seafood Hotpot   Yosenabe

5 oz (150 g) each of any of the following seafood ingredients: fresh shrimp; clams; shucked oysters; scallops; and fish fillets
5 oz (150 g) chicken fillets (optional)
1 packet (3½ oz/100 g) dried *shirataki* or bean thread noodles
1 small carrot, peeled and sliced
½ small Chinese cabbage
1 bunch chrysanthemum greens
2 leeks, white part only, cut diagonally
12 fresh shiitake mushrooms, stems discarded, caps cross-cut
4 oz (125 g) *enokitake* mushrooms
1 cake (8 oz/250 g) soft tofu, cubed
Ponzu Dipping Sauce (page 24)
Japanese soy sauce, to serve

Stock
7 cups (1¾ liters) Basic Dashi Stock (page 23) or 4 teaspoons *dashi* stock granules dissolved in 7 cups (1¾ liters) hot water
4–5 tablespoons Japanese soy sauce
2 tablespoons *mirin*
8 oz (250 g) daikon radish (about 4 in/ 10 cm), peeled and sliced

1 Prepare the Stock by placing all ingredients in a large pan and simmer on medium heat for 15 minutes. Set aside and keep warm.
2 Peel and devein the shrimp, keeping the heads and tails intact. Scrub the clams clean and soak in lightly salted water for 20 minutes. Rinse the oysters thoroughly with lightly salted water. Drain in a colander and set aside. Slice the fish fillets into bite-sized pieces. Blanch the fish quickly in boiling water until it just changes color, then drain and set aside.
3 Slice the chicken fillets into bite-sized pieces and blanch in boiling water and leave to chill in a small bowl of ice water. Drain, rinse in cold water, drain again and set aside.
4 Cook the noodles in boiling water until soft (see packet instructions). Drain and set aside. Blanch the carrot and cabbage. Drain and set aside. Wash the chrysanthemum greens, discard the hard stems and cut them into lengths. Arrange all the ingredients attractively on a large platter.
5 Pour the Stock into a heat-proof casserole and set it on a hotplate or gas burner at the center of the table. To cook, place the chicken and clams in the Stock, followed by half of the fish, shrimp, oysters, noodles and vegetables. Wait until the ingredients are cooked, before adding the remaining ingredients. Serve with Ponzu Dipping Sauce (page 24) and Japanese soy sauce.

Note: Very fresh seabream, salmon, snapper or mackerel fillets are ideal for this dish.

Serves 6   Preparation time: 45 mins   Cooking time: 30 mins

Green Tea Ice Cream   Matcha Aisukuriimu

A popular summertime dessert in Japanese restaurants, this might be termed a "modern classic." Finely powdered green tea gives a uniquely Japanese flavor to this delightfully rich ice cream.

2¼ oz (75 g) green tea powder
⅓ cup (75 ml) cognac or brandy
5 cups (1¼ liters) fresh milk
1 cup (250 ml) heavy cream
1⅓ cups (100 g) skimmed milk
 powder
1¾ cups (350 g) sugar
Sweetened *azuki* beans, to serve
 (optional)

1 Place the green tea powder in a bowl, add the cognac and mix well.
2 Pour the fresh milk, cream, milk powder and sugar into another bowl and mix well. Transfer to a saucepan and bring to a boil over moderate heat. Remove from the heat and allow to cool to a lukewarm temperature, then add the green tea mixture and mix well.
3 Chill immediately in the freezer portion of the refrigerator until ice crystals start to form around the edges of the container. Pour the mixture into a blender or food processor and blend for a few seconds to break up the crystals. Leave the mixture to freeze in a plastic container. For an interesting variation, serve the ice cream topped with sweetened *azuki* beans.

Note: Alternatively, pour the cooked mixture (Step 2) into a one-gallon ice-cream maker and freeze according to the manufacturer's instructions.

Makes 5 pints (2½ liters)   Preparation time: 10 mins   Cooking time: 10 mins

Tomato Cognac Sorbet   Tomato Burandi-Fumi

A curious sounding dessert, this modern Japanese creation is simple to make, visually appealing and surprisingly good to eat.

4 large ripe tomatoes
3 cups (750 ml) water
½ oz (100 g) sugar or slightly more,
 to taste
1 teaspoon salt
2 tablespoons cognac or brandy, or
 more to taste

1 Blanch the tomatoes in a large pan of boiling water for about 15 seconds, remove and place in cold water. As soon as the tomatoes are cool enough to handle, peel.
2 Pour the water, sugar and salt into a large saucepan and bring to a boil. Add the tomatoes and simmer gently until they are tender. Remove from the heat, add the cognac and leave to cool.
3 Blend the tomatoes and the cognac. Transfer the mixture to the freezer container of a one-gallon ice-cream maker and freeze according to the manufacturer's instructions. Scoop into chilled serving cups to serve.

Note: Alternatively, you can serve the tomatoes whole. Refrigerate until just before serving. Dish the tomatoes into chilled, individual glass bowls with a little syrup.

Serves 2–4   Preparation time: 15 mins   Cooking time: 25 mins

Red Bean Pancakes   Dora-Yaki

Very popular in Japan and sold hot at stalls everywhere, these pancakes can be found with a variety of fillings, including Western-style custard. *Azuki* bean is however the traditional favorite. Sweetened *azuki* bean paste is also known as "sweetened red bean paste."

2 cups (300 g) cornstarch
4 teaspoons sugar
1 cup (250 ml) water
1 egg white, beaten until fluffy
Oil, to grease pan
1 cup (7 oz/200 g) Sweetened Azuki
  Bean Paste (below)

1 Sift the cornstarch into a bowl and add the sugar. Stir in the water to make a smooth batter, then fold in the egg white. Heat a frying pan and grease lightly with oil. Drop about 1½ tablespoons of the batter into the pan, letting it spread by itself. When tiny bubbles begin to form on the pancake surface, turn over. Fry for 30 seconds, then remove. Make another pancake in the same fashion. Spread 1 heaped teaspoon of the *azuki* bean paste onto one pancake and cover with the second pancake. Repeat until all the batter is used up.

Makes 20   Preparation time: 10 mins   Cooking time: 30 mins

Sweetened Azuki Bean Paste

4 oz (125 g) dried *azuki* beans
½ cup (100 g) sugar
Pinch of salt

1 Boil the *azuki* beans in water to cover, then lower the heat to medium and continue cooking until the wrinkles on the bean skin have disappeared. Drain the beans, and pour in three times as much water as beans and return to a boil. Then simmer over medium-low heat until the beans are very tender. Drain the beans in a colander lined with a dish towel. To further remove excess moisture, gather the ends of the towel and squeeze out the water. Transfer the beans to a blender or food processor and process to a smooth paste.
2 Place the paste in a saucepan, add the sugar and salt, and cook over medium heat, stirring constantly with a wooden spoon until the paste thickens. Remove the pot from the heat, stir to cool and freeze or store in the refrigerator for not more than a week.

Makes 1½ cups   Preparation time: 5 mins   Cooking time: 1 hour

Jellied Plums   Kingyoku-Kan

A simple but decorative dessert, with large grapes or plums set in jellied plum wine (*umeshu*). If Japanese plum wine is not available, substitute with any other fortified fruit wine, such as peach or raspberry.

8 large seedless grapes or small
  plums
2½ envelopes (25 g) unflavored
  Japanese gelatin powder
¼ cup (60 ml) water
1 small bottle Japanese plum wine
  (*umeshu*) (1⅔ cups/420 ml)
  or substitute (see above)
2½ tablespoons sugar
1 teaspoon cognac or brandy
8 porcelain teacups or jelly molds

1 Blanch the grapes or plums in hot water for about 10 seconds, drain and put in cold water to chill for a few seconds. Peel, halve and set aside.
2 Stir the gelatin and water in a non-reactive saucepan. Simmer over medium heat, stirring constantly, until the gelatin is dissolved and smooth. Add the plum wine and sugar, stir until the sugar is melted. Remove from the heat, add the cognac and stir.
3 Portion the grapes or plums into the teacups. Pour the liquid jelly into the teacups and chill until the jelly sets.

Serves 4   Preparation time: 10 mins   Cooking time: 10 mins

Lily Bulb Dumplings Chakin-Shibori

The sweet, nutty flavor and smooth texture of lily bulbs, which are readily available in Japan during the winter months, go well with a red bean filling in these quickly made dumplings. You may substitute lily bulbs with sweet potatoes—for the best results, use the yellow-fleshed variety.

14 oz (400 g) lily bulbs or sweet
  potatoes
¼ cup (50 g) sugar
4 tablespoons Sweetened Azuki
  Bean Paste (page 107)
2 tablespoons finely grated *yuzu*
  orange or lemon peel

1 Separate the lily bulb, which looks somewhat like a head of garlic, into petals. Place the petals on a plate and steam for about 3 minutes or until soft, then drain. If using sweet potatoes, steam them whole until they are soft, then drain and peel.
2 Mash the steamed vegetable, then mix with the sugar and knead well. Flatten about 2 tablespoons of the purée, and spread a teaspoon of *azuki* bean paste on it. Shape the purée into a ball, then wrap the ball in a cloth and squeeze gently at the top to form a dumpling. Remove from the cloth and sprinkle with a little of the grated peel. Repeat until all the purée is used up, then serve.

Serves 4–6   Preparation time: 10 mins   Cooking time: 35 mins

Cherry Blossom Dumplings Sakura Mochi

Wrapped in cherry leaves, these dumplings filled with sweet *azuki* bean paste are inevitably associated with the springtime cherry blossom or sakura season. If you cannot find edible cherry leaves packed in brine, the dumplings can be served without them.

1 cup (150 g) cornstarch
2 teaspoons sugar
½ cup (125 ml) water
½ egg white, beaten until fluffy
Pinch of salt
Oil, to grease pan lightly
½ cup (3½ oz/100 g) Sweetened
  Azuki Bean Paste (page 107)
5 cherry blossom leaves or other
  leaves, to garnish

1 Sift the cornstarch into a bowl and add the sugar. Add the water, a little at a time and stir well to dissolve the sugar. Fold in the egg white and salt. Lightly grease a skillet and place over low heat.
2 Pour in one-fifth of the batter and spread to form an oval shape. Cook until the top of the pancake becomes dry and then turn over. Cook the other side but do not allow the pancake to brown. Remove the pancake and spread one heaped tablespoon of the Sweetened Azuki Bean Paste evenly on it. Fold over to make a dumpling and garnish with a cherry blossom leaf. Repeat until all the batter is used up.

Serves 4   Preparation time: 10 mins   Cooking time: 5 mins

Measurements and conversions

Measurements in this book are given in volume as far as possible. Teaspoon, tablespoon and cup measurements should be level, not heaped, unless otherwise indicated. Australian readers please note that the standard Australian measuring spoon is larger than the UK or American spoon by 5 ml, so use ¾ tablespoon instead of a full tablespoon when following the recipes.

Liquid Conversions

Imperial	Metric	US cups
½ fl oz	15 ml	1 tablespoon
1 fl oz	30 ml	⅛ cup
2 fl oz	60 ml	¼ cup
3 fl oz	85 ml	⅓ cup
4 fl oz	125 ml	½ cup
5 fl oz	150 ml	⅔ cup
6 fl oz	175 ml	¾ cup
8 fl oz	250 ml	1 cup
12 fl oz	375 ml	1½ cups
16 fl oz	500 ml	2 cups
	1 liter	4 cups

Note:
1 UK pint = 20 fl oz
1 US pint = 16 fl oz

Solid Weight Conversions

Imperial	Metric
½ oz	15 g
1 oz	28 g
1½ oz	45 g
2 oz	60 g
3 oz	85 g
3½ oz	100 g
4 oz (¼ lb)	125 g
5 oz	150 g
6 oz	175 g
7 oz	200 g
8 oz (½ lb)	225 g
9 oz	260 g
10 oz	300 g
16 oz (1 lb)	450 g
32 oz (2 lbs)	1 kg

Oven Temperatures

Heat	Fahrenheit	Centigrade/Celsius	British Gas Mark
Very cool	230	110	¼
Cool or slow	275–300	135–150	1–2
Moderate	350	175	4
Hot	425	220	7
Very hot	450	230	8

Index of recipes

Mail-order/online sources

The ingredients used in this book can all be found in markets featuring the foods of Japan. Many of them can also be found in any well-stocked supermarket. Ingredients not found locally may be available from the mail-order/online resources listed below.

Central Market (Austin North Lamar)
4001 North Lamar Boulevard
Austin, TX 78756, USA
Tel: (512) 206 1000
centralmarket.com

Central Market (Dallas Preston Royal)
10720 Preston Rd.
Dallas, TX 75230, USA
Tel: (972) 860 6500
centralmarket.com

Central Market (Houston)
3815 Westheimer Rd
Houston, TX 77027, USA
Tel: (713) 386 1700
centralmarket.com

Central Market (Southlake)
1425 E. Southlake Blvd.
Southlake, TX 76092, USA
Tel: 817-310-5600
centralmarket.com

Frieda's Inc
4465 Corporate Center Drive
Los Alamitos CA 90720, USA
friedas.com

Fuji Mart Melbourne
34 Elizabeth St, 3141 South Yarra
Victoria, Australia
Tel: (3) 9826 5839
junpacific.com/e/fujimart-vic

House of Spices (India) Inc
127-40 Willets Point Blvd.
Flushing, NY 11368
Telephone: (718) 507-4600
customerservice@houseofspicesindia.com
hosindia.com

Ichiban Kan
22 Peace Plaza #540
East Mall 2nd Floor (Between Post &
Laguna)
San Francisco, CA 94115, USA
Tel: (415) 409-0472
ichibankanusa.com

New Kam Man
200 Canal Street
New York, NY 10079, USA
Tel: (212) 571 0330
info@newkamman.com
newkamman.com

Pacific Mercantile Company, Inc
1925 Lawrence St, Denver,
CO 80202, USA
Tel: (303) 295 0293
info@pacificmercantile.com
pacificeastwest.com

The Spice House (Milwaukee, WI)
1031 North Old World 3rd St
Milwaukee WI 53203, USA
Tel: 414-272-0977
thespicehouse.com

The Spice House (Chicago, IL)
1512 North Wells St
Chicago IL 60610, USA
Tel: (312) 274 0378
thespicehouse.com

The Spice House (Evanston, IL)
1941 Central Street
Evanston IL 60201, USA
Tel: (847) 328 3711
thespicehouse.com

Uwajimaya (Seattle)
600 5th Avenue South
Seattle, WA 98104, USA
Tel: (206) 624-6248
SeattleStore@uwajimaya.com
uwajimaya.com

Uwajimaya (Renton)
501 South Grady Way
Renton, WA 98057, USA
Tel: (206) 624-6248
RentonStore@uwajimaya.com
uwajimaya.com